THE LOST PRINCESS OF OZ

ILLUSTRATED BY

JOHN R. NEILL

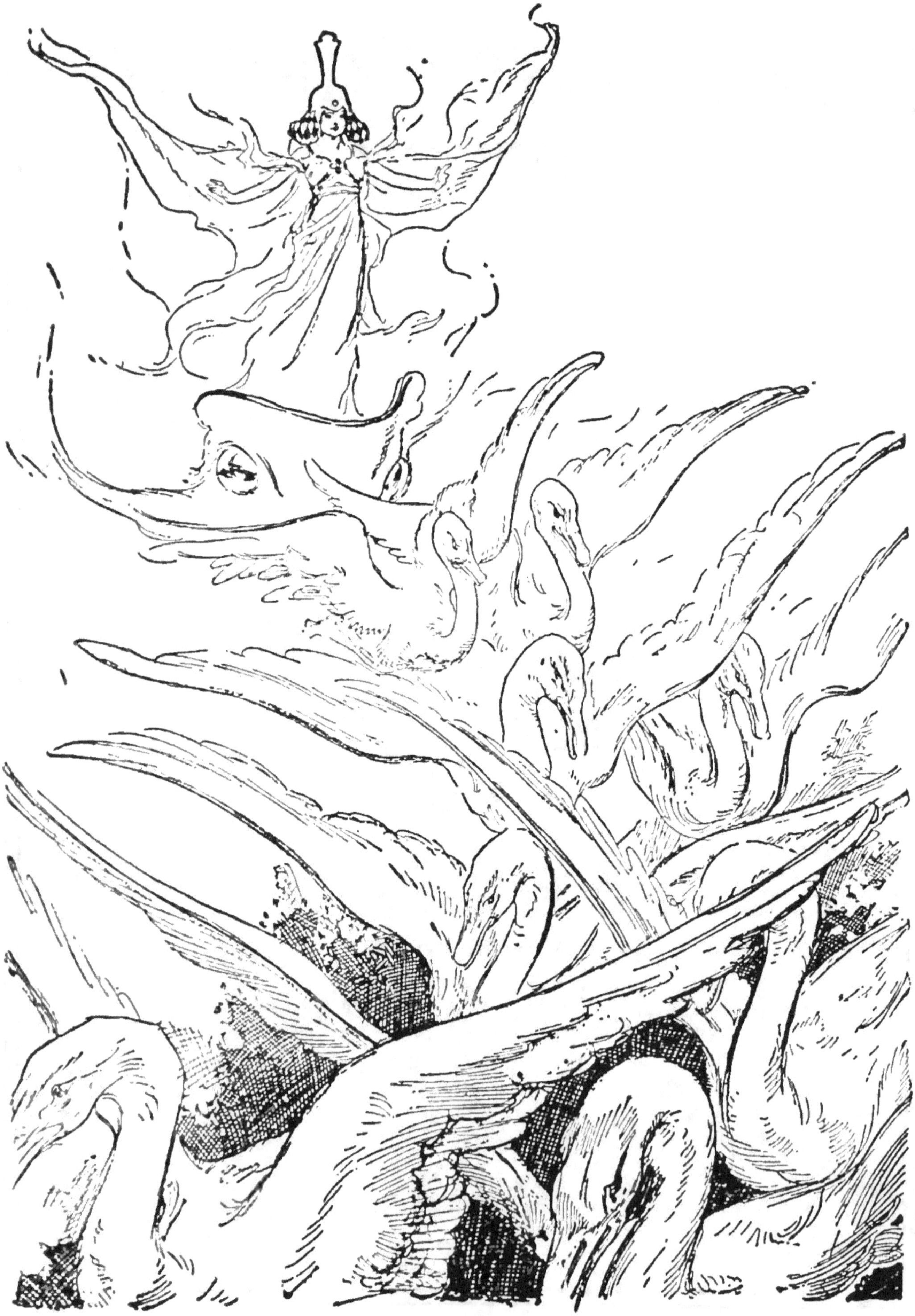

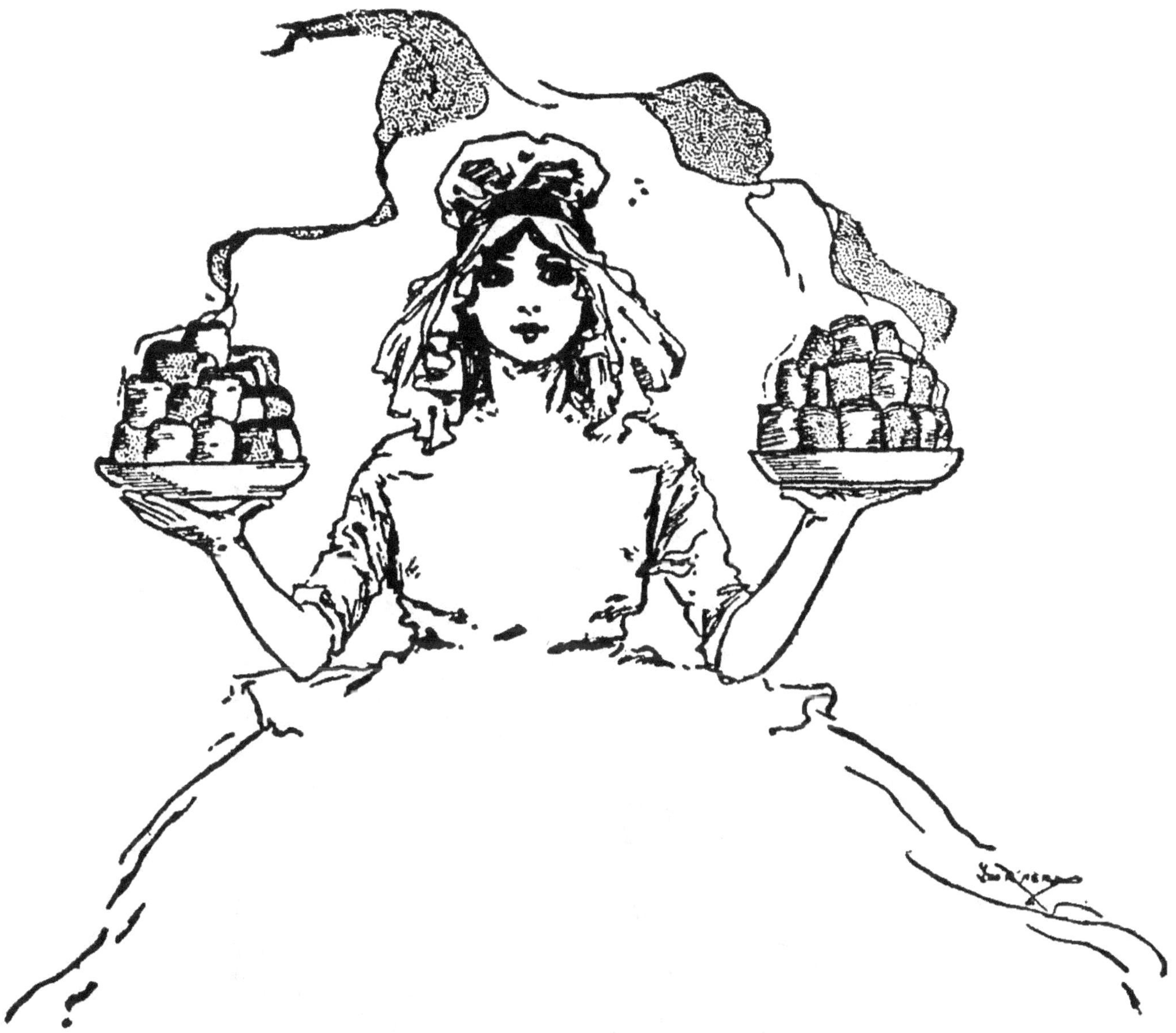

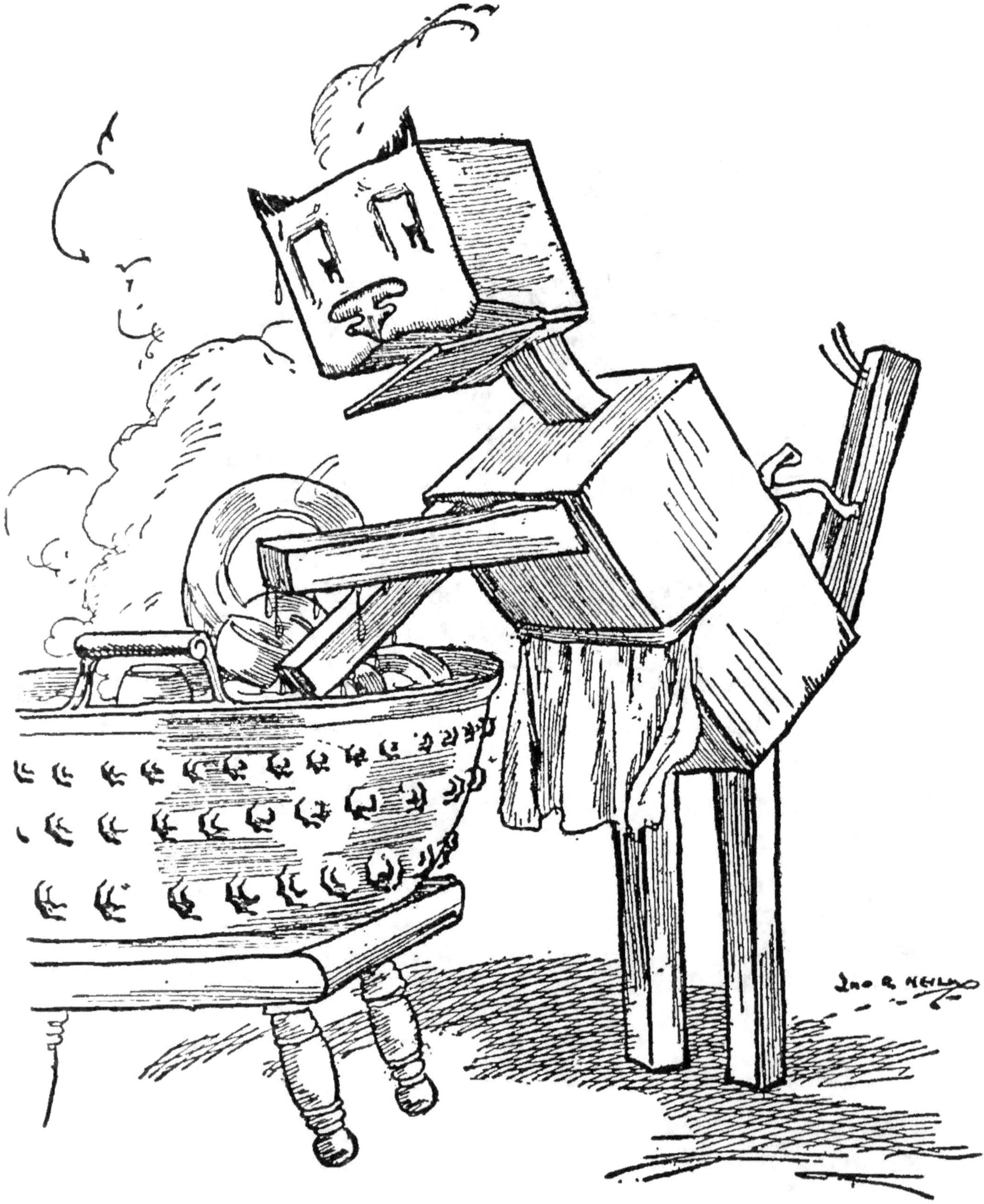
JNO R NEILL

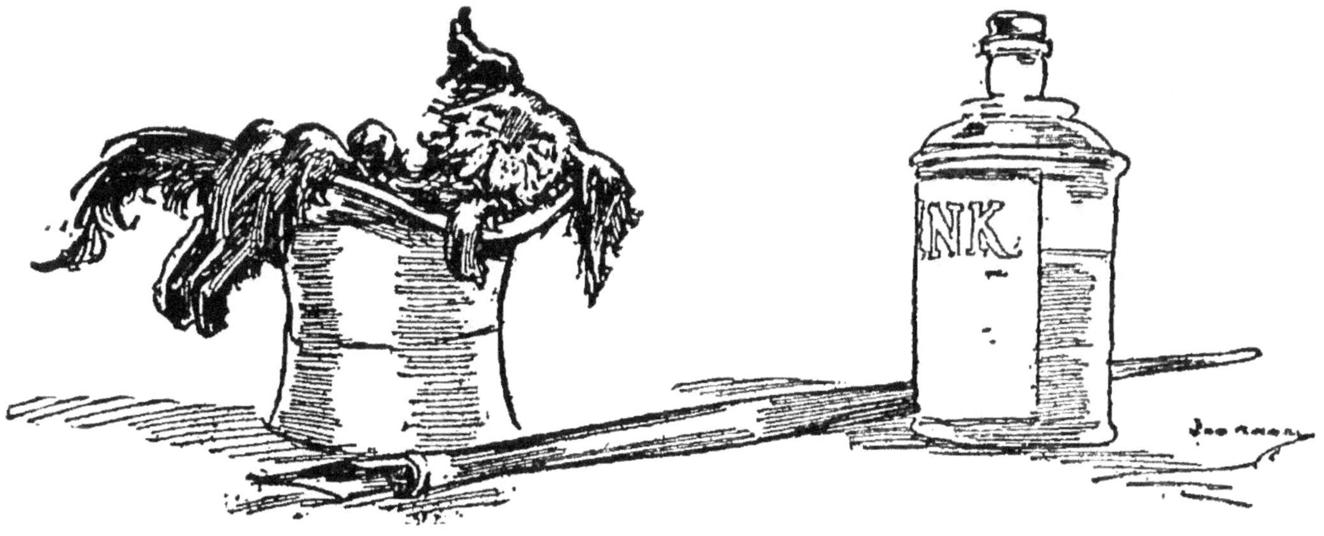
INK

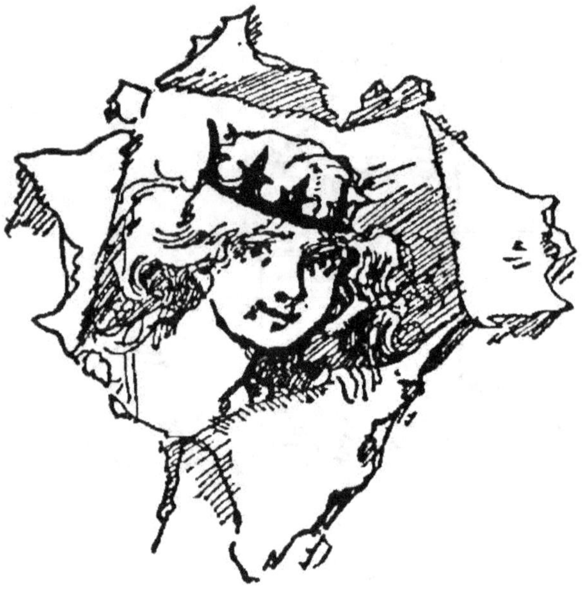

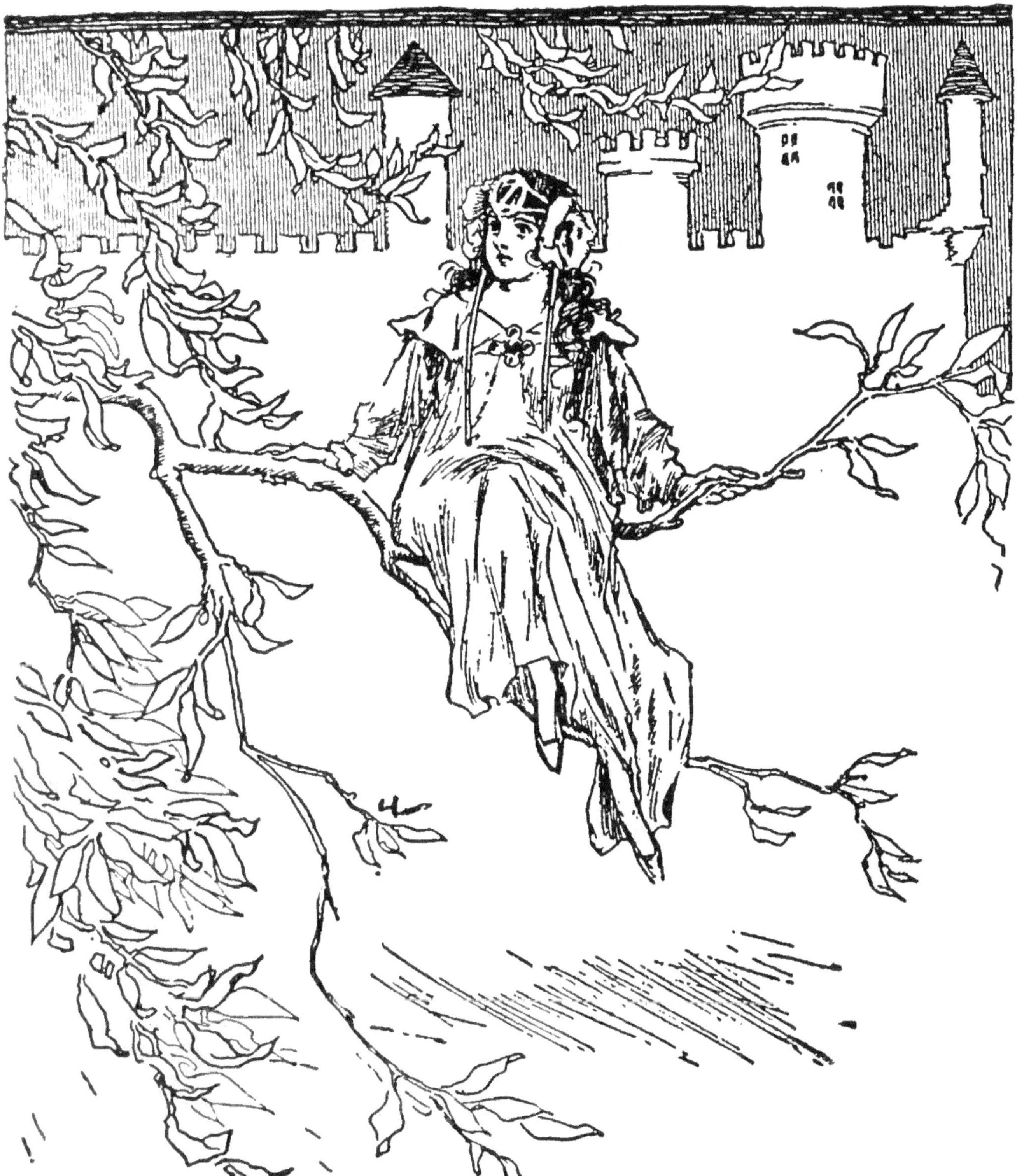

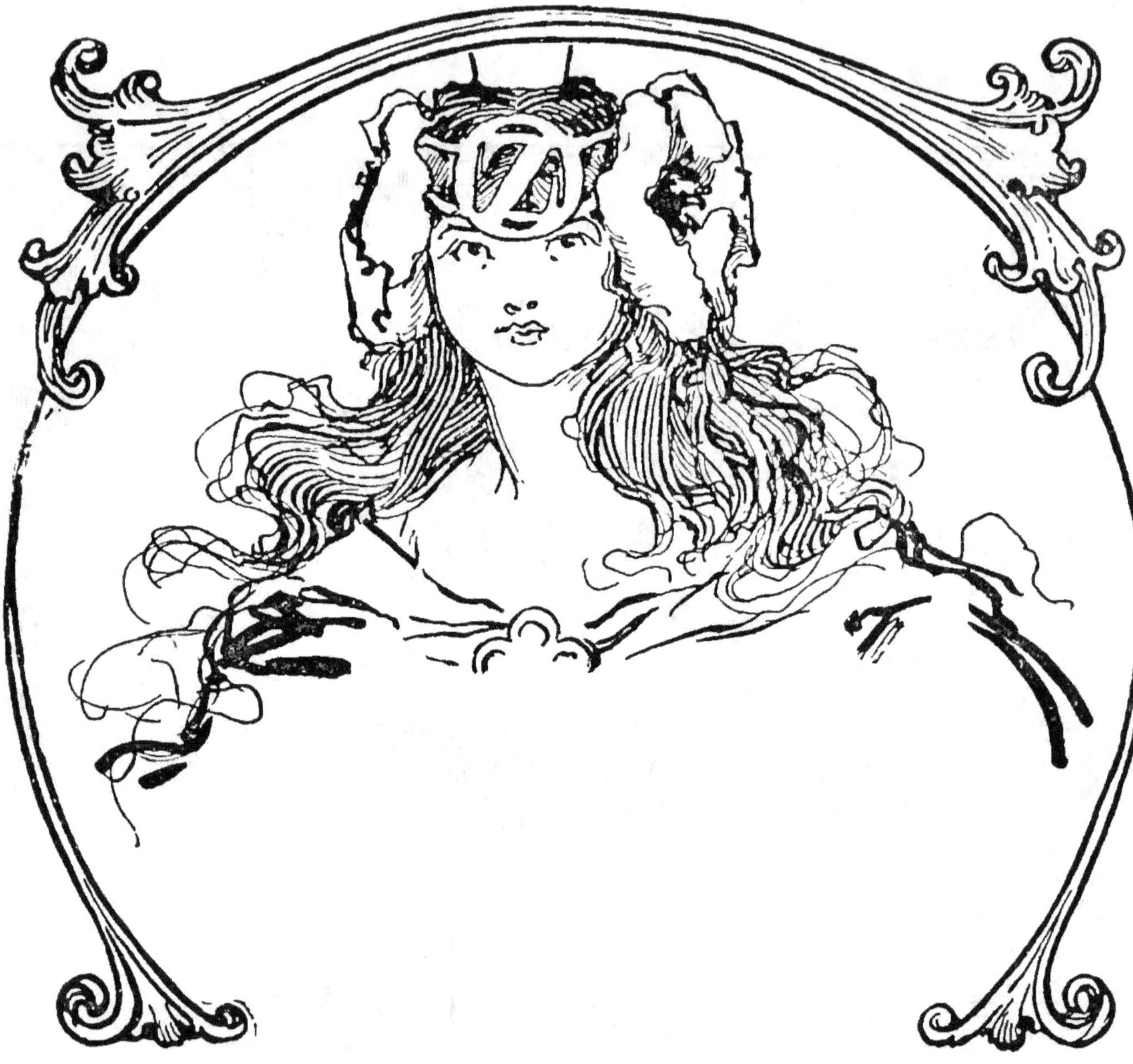

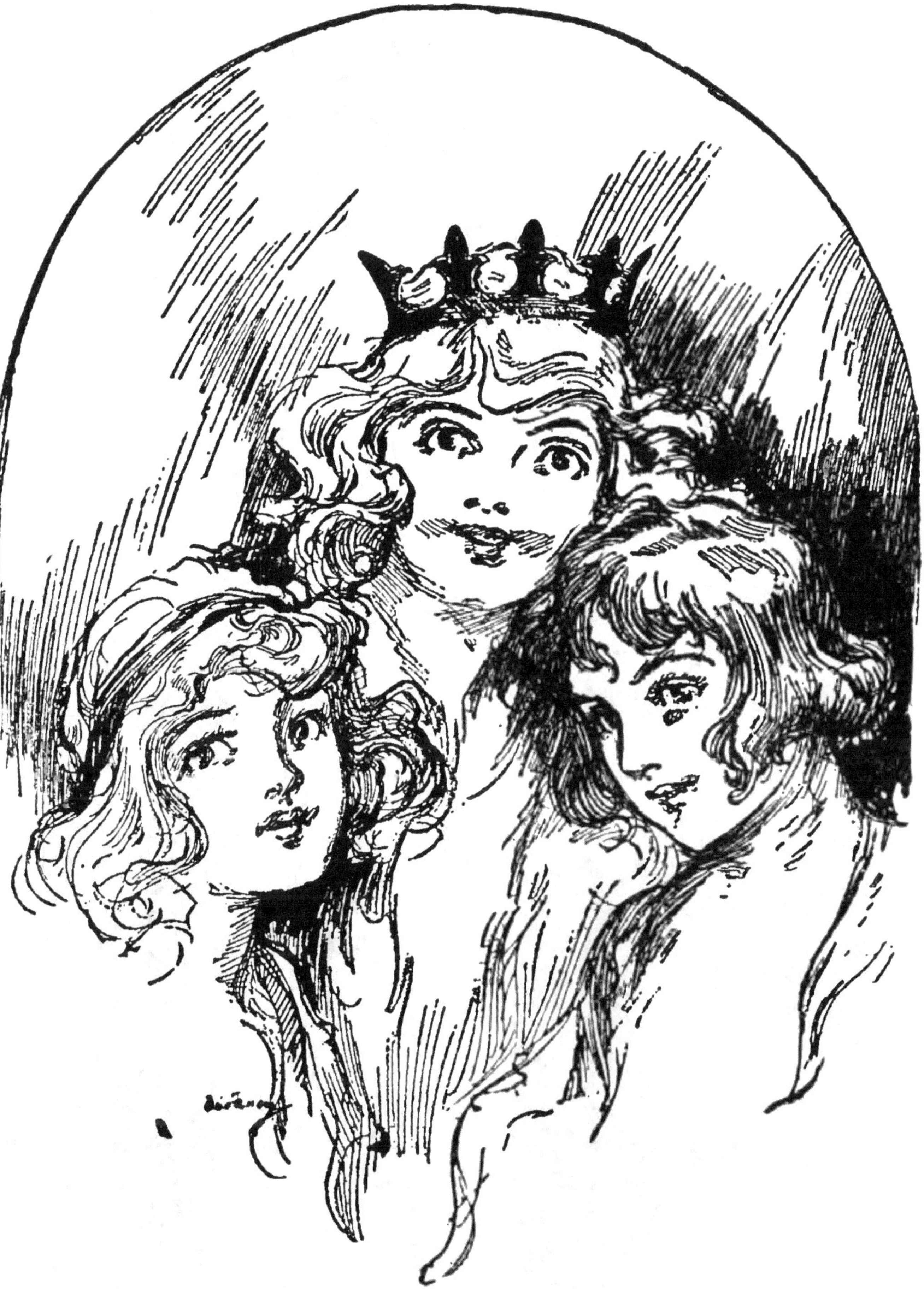

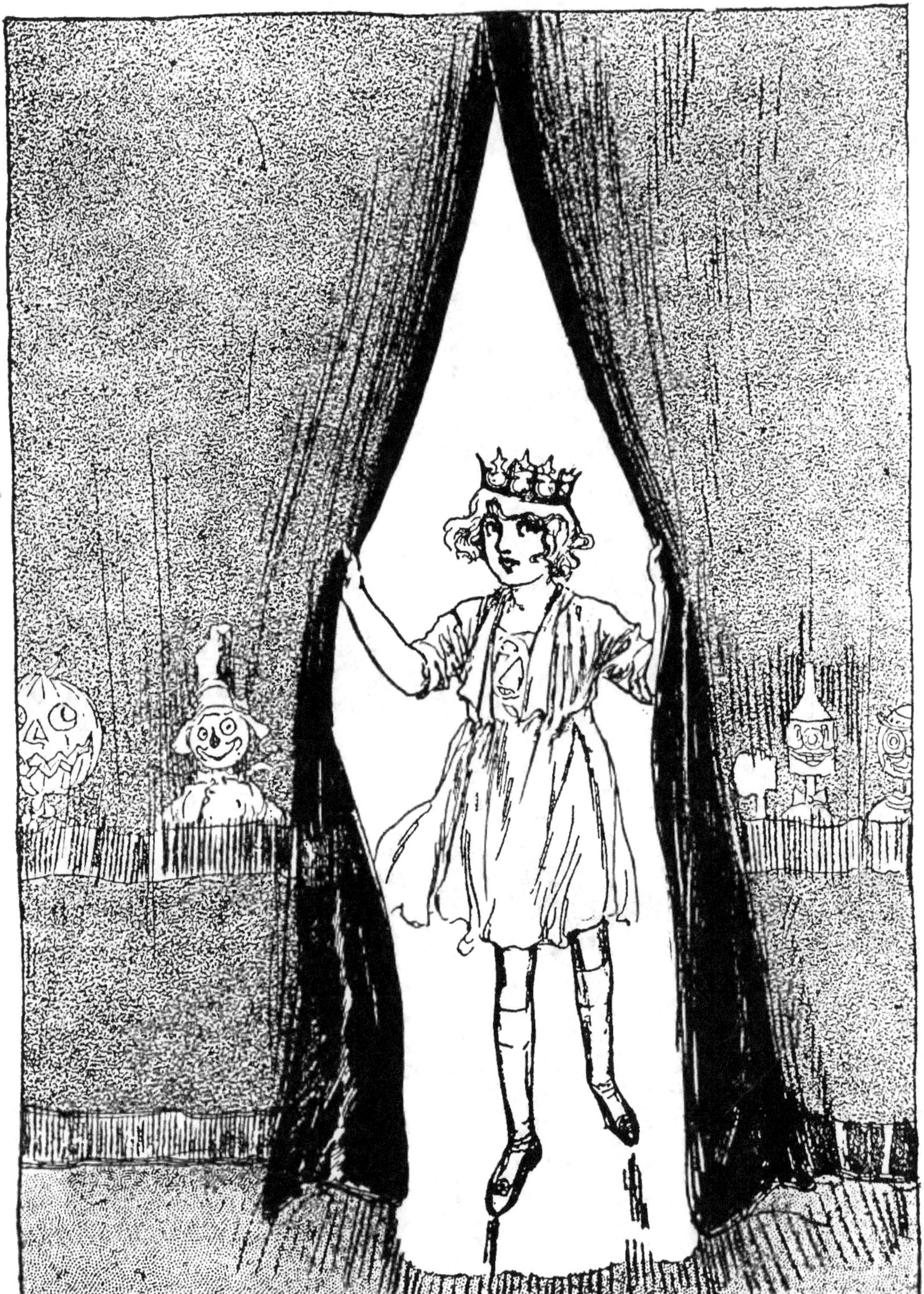

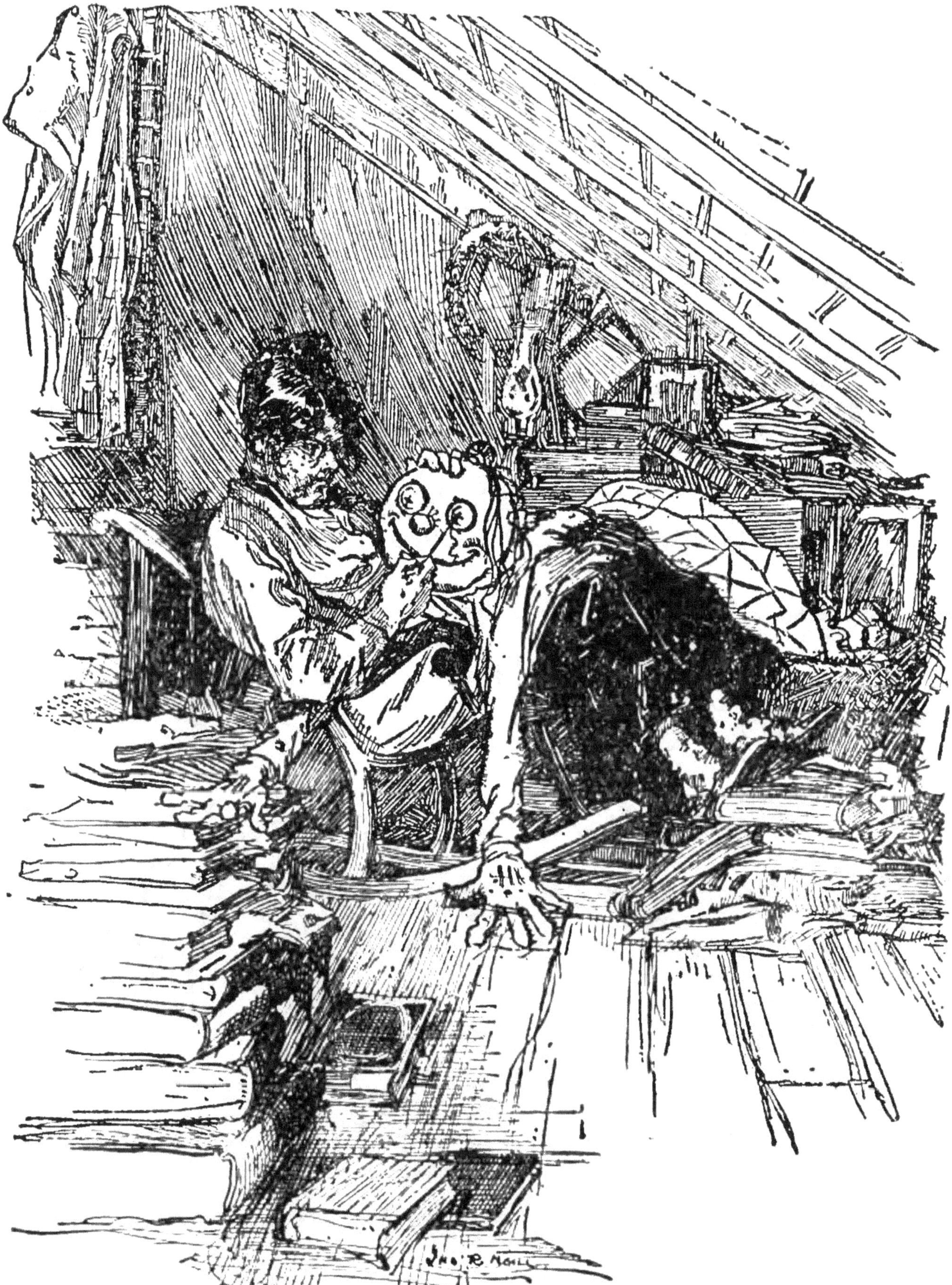

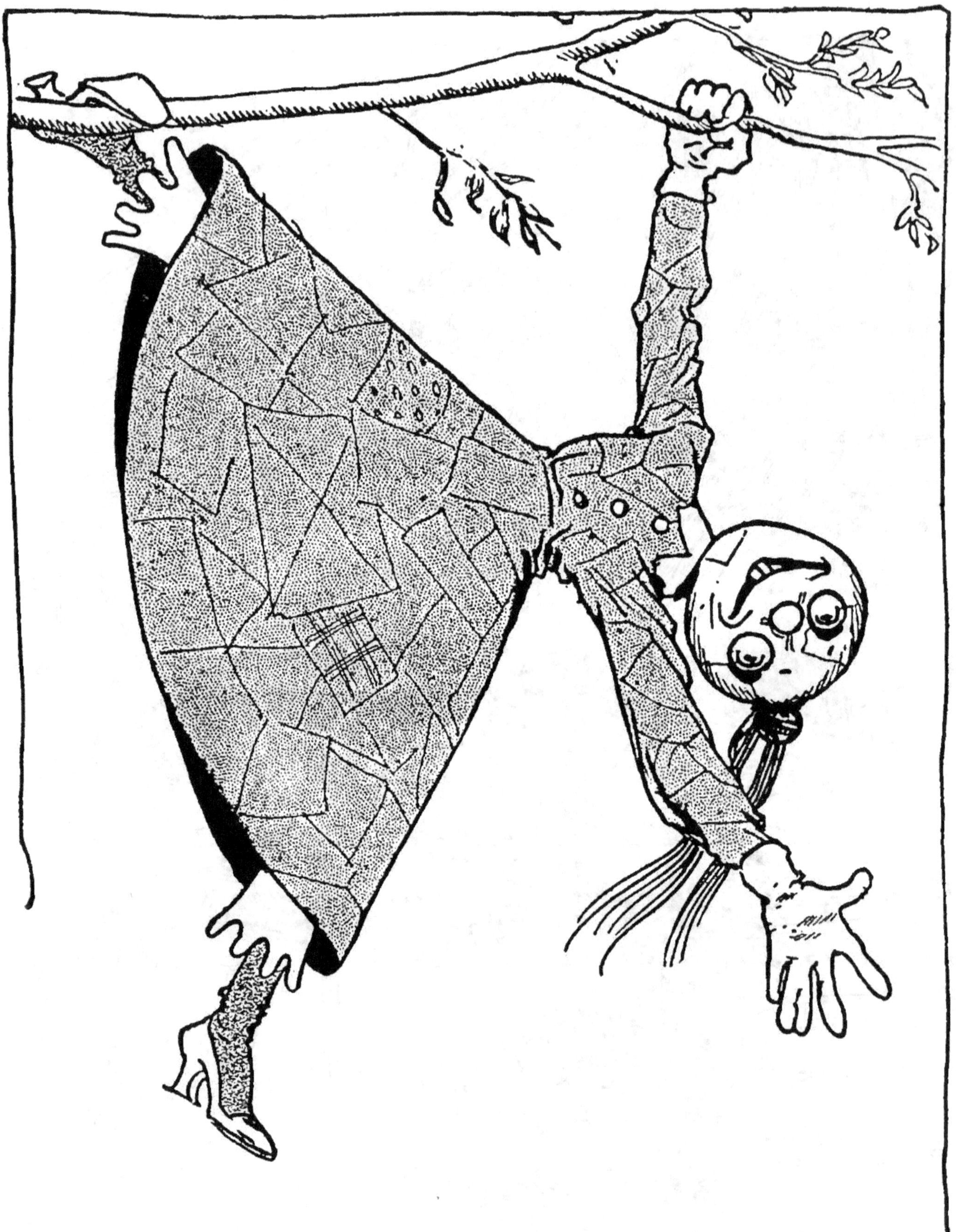

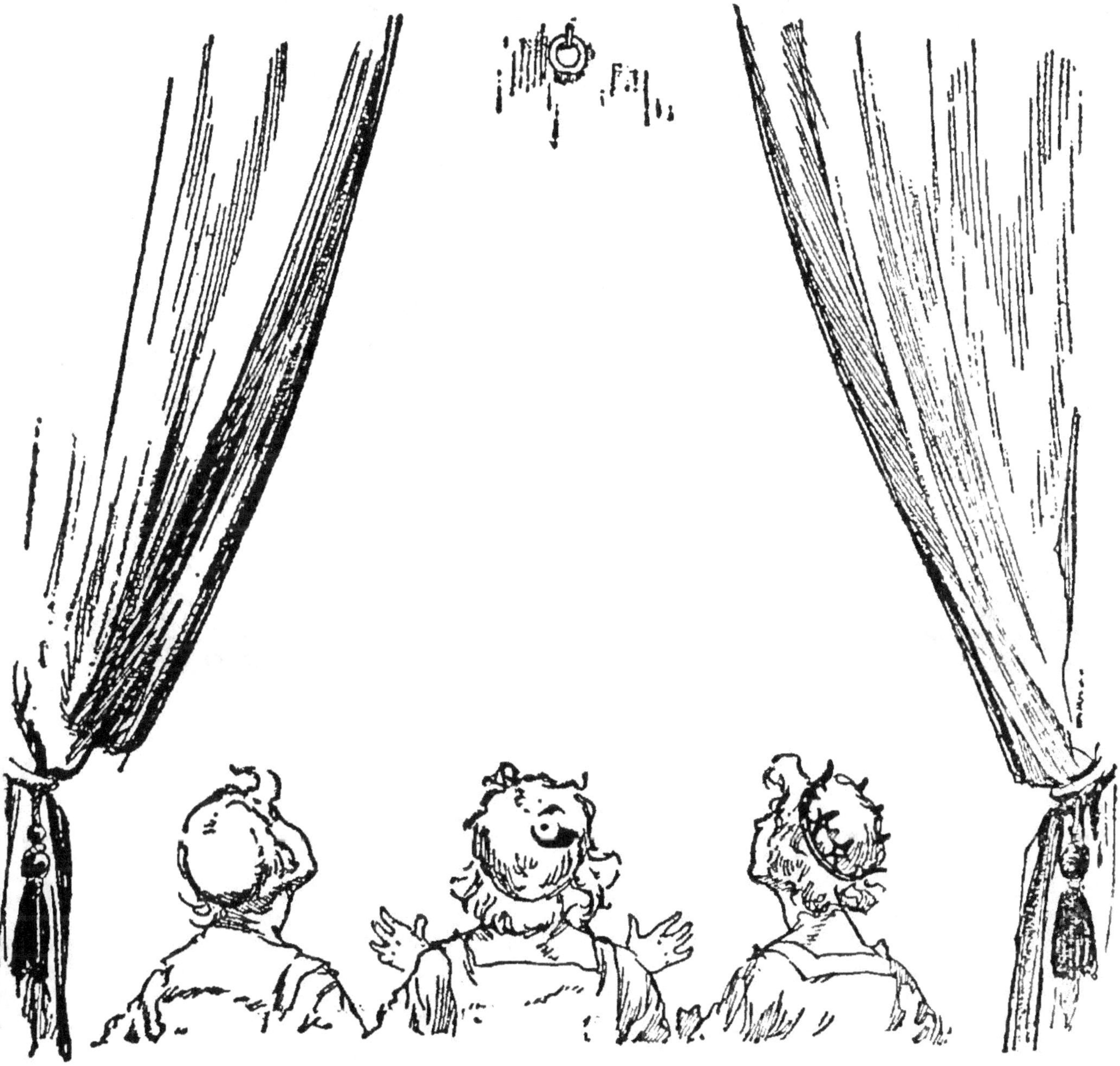

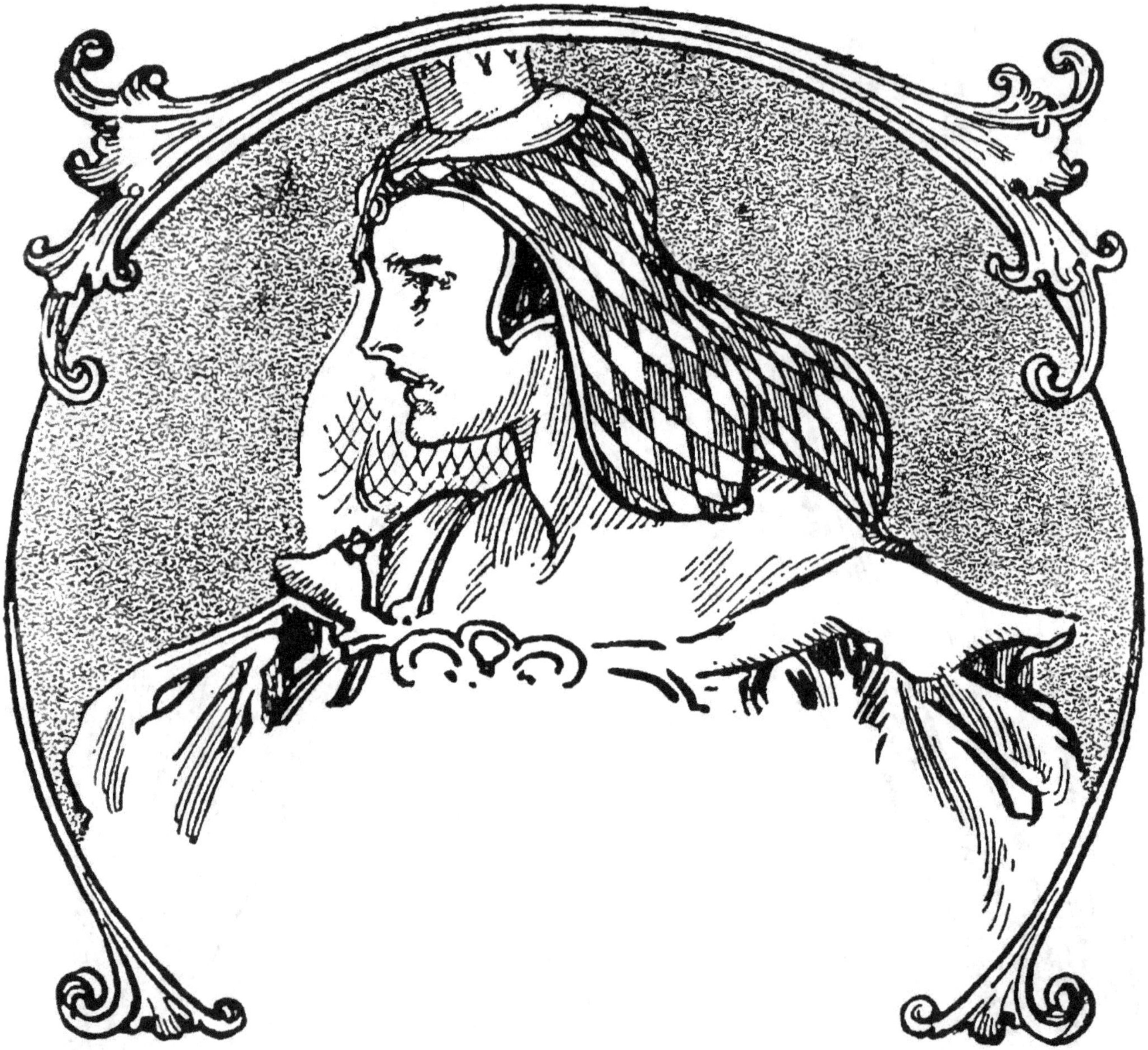

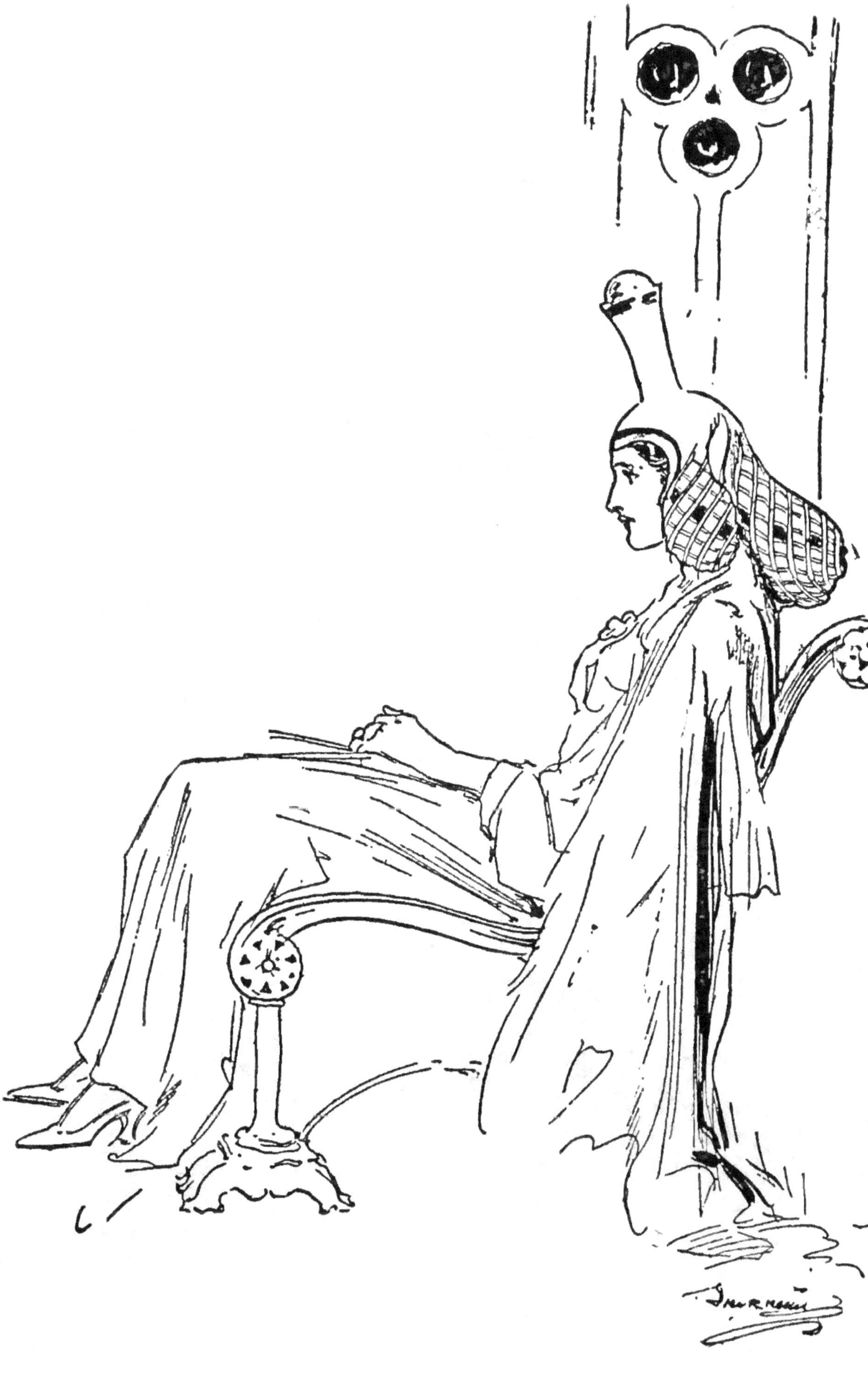

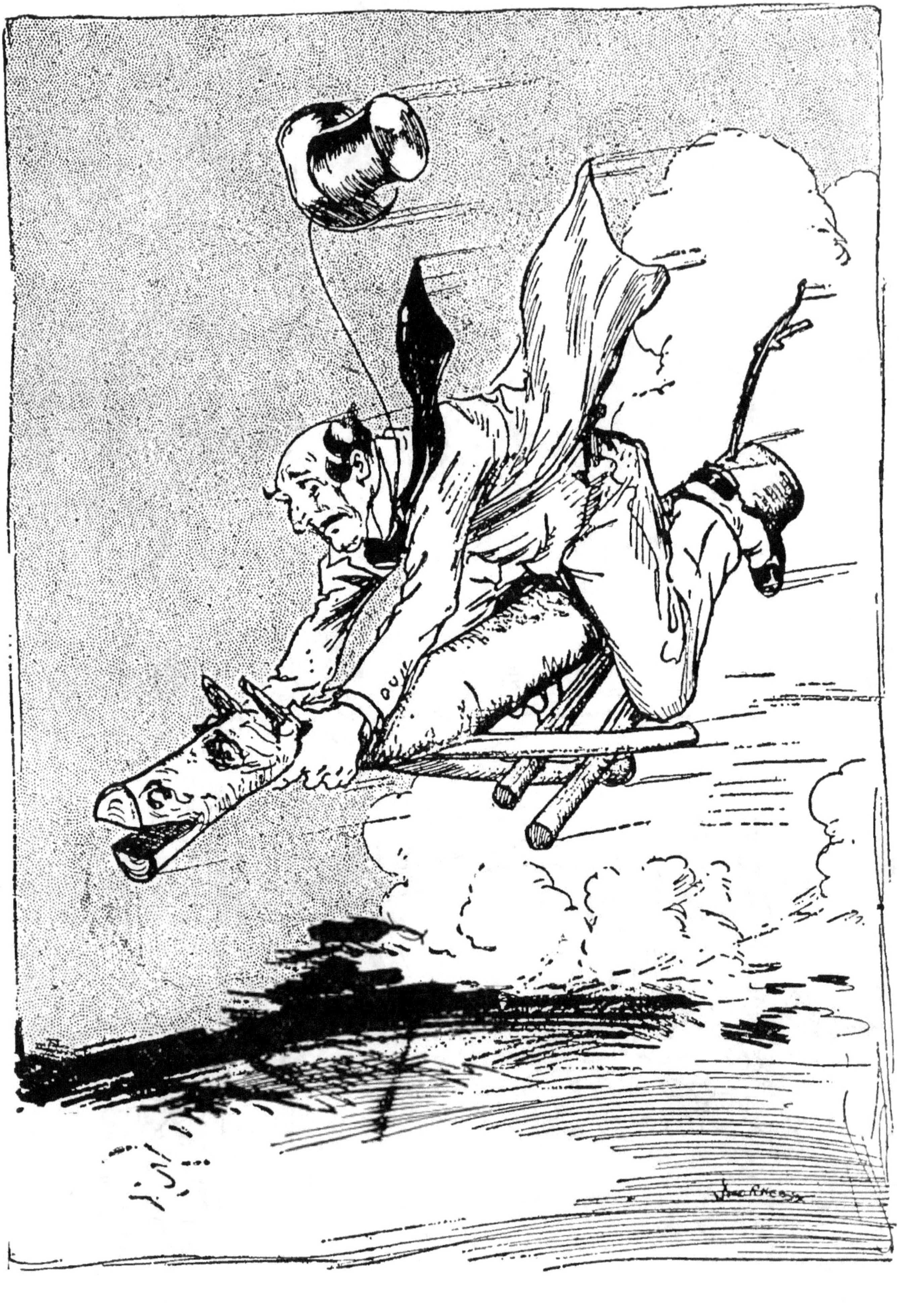

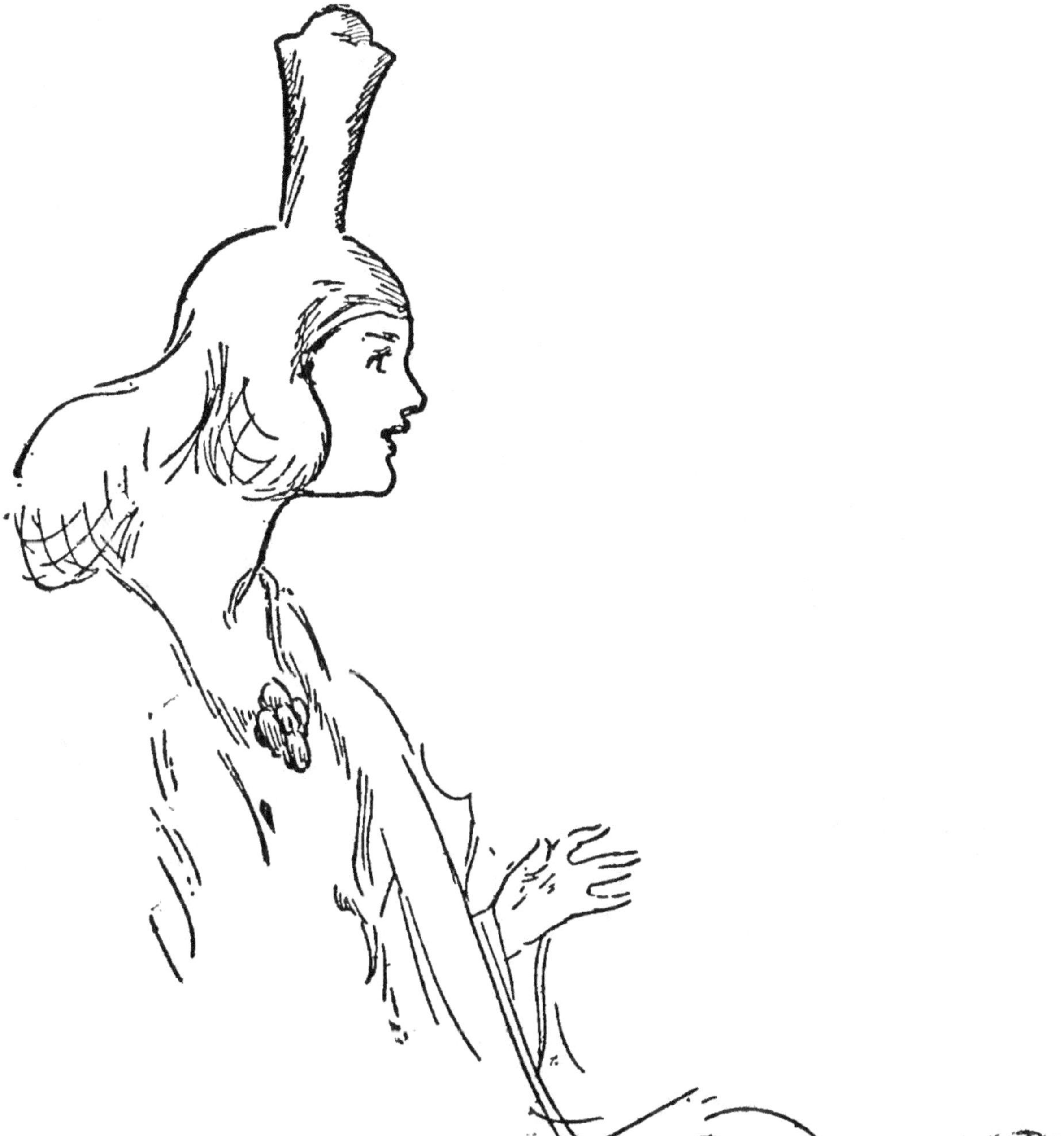

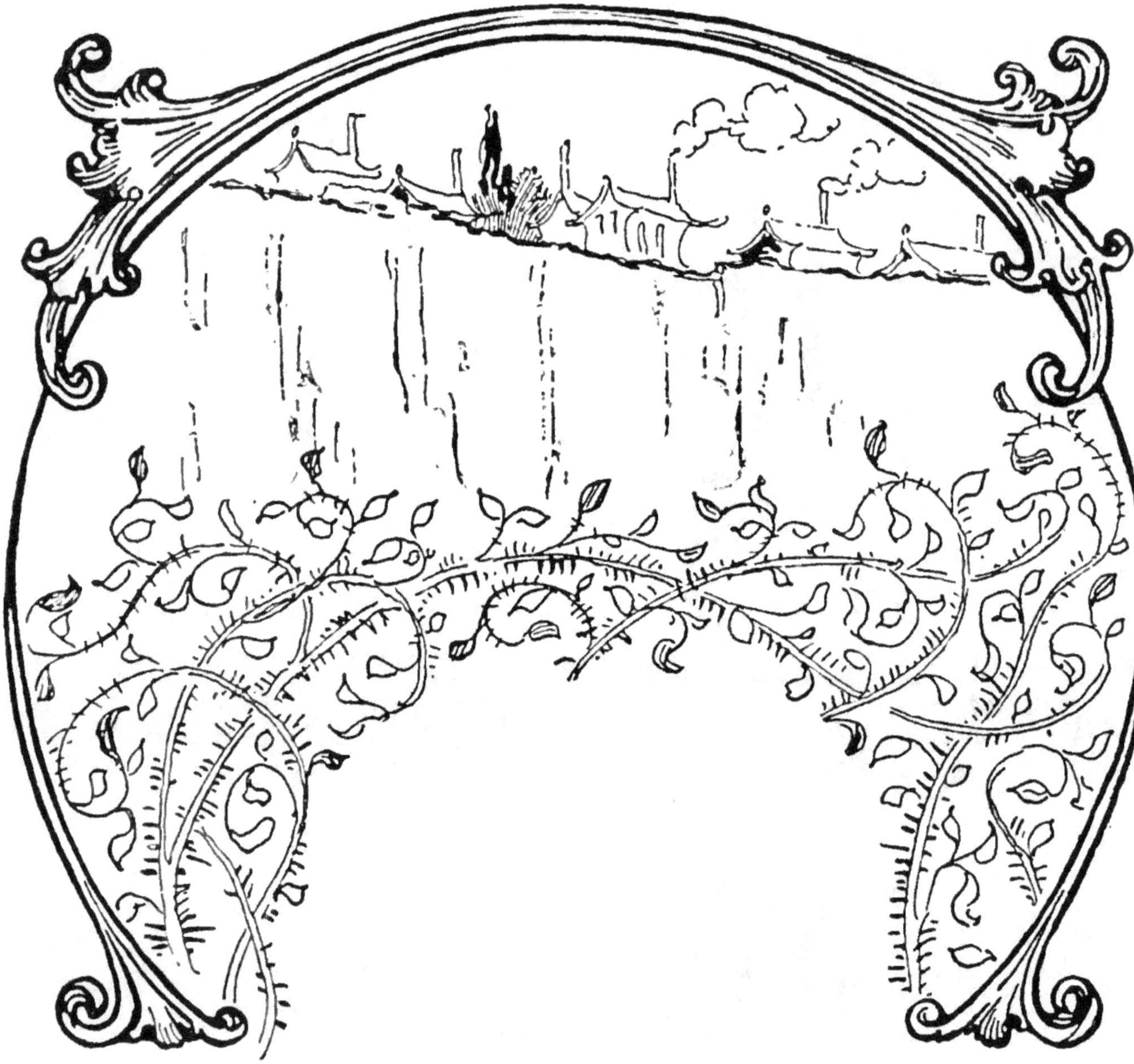

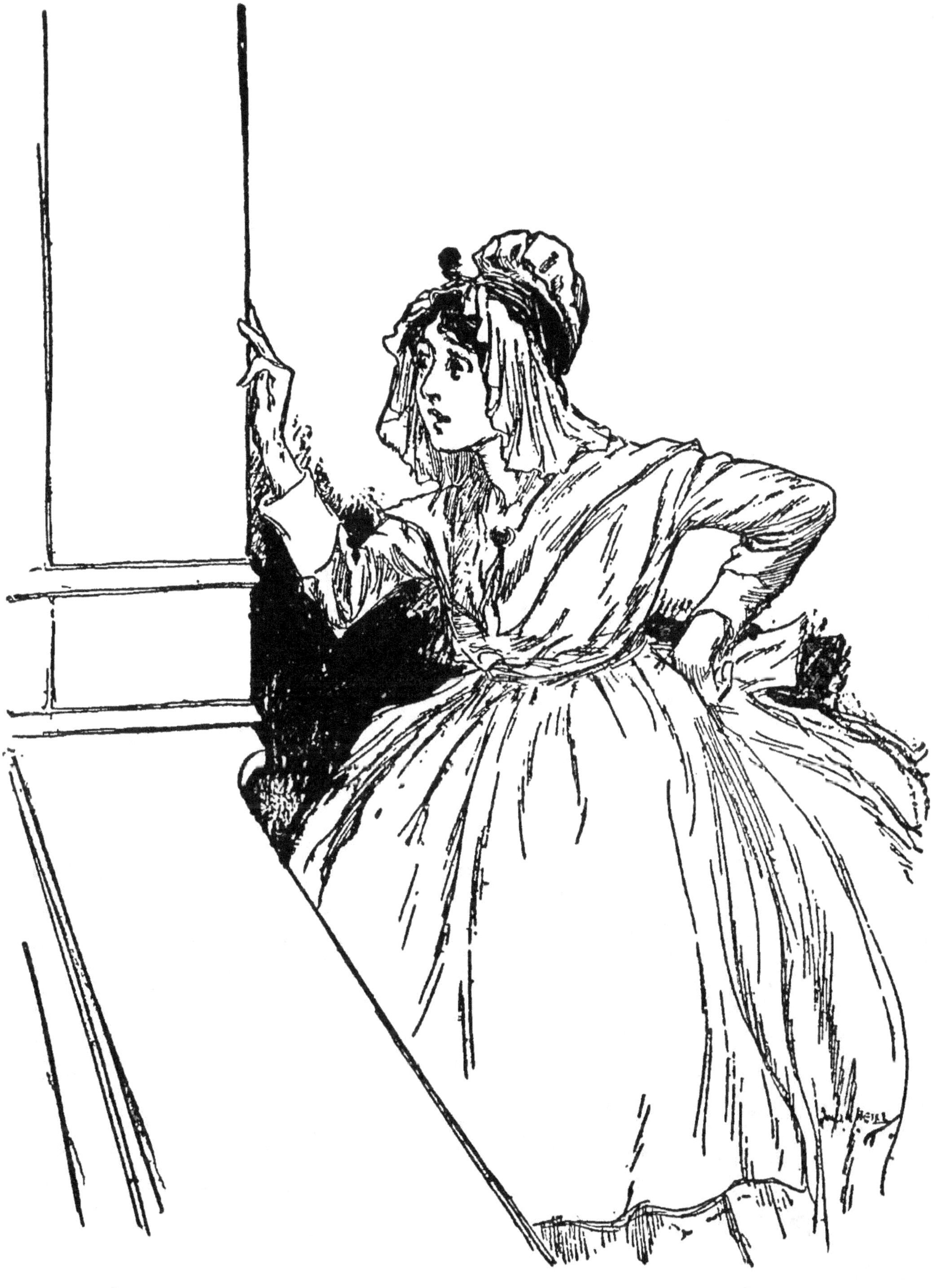

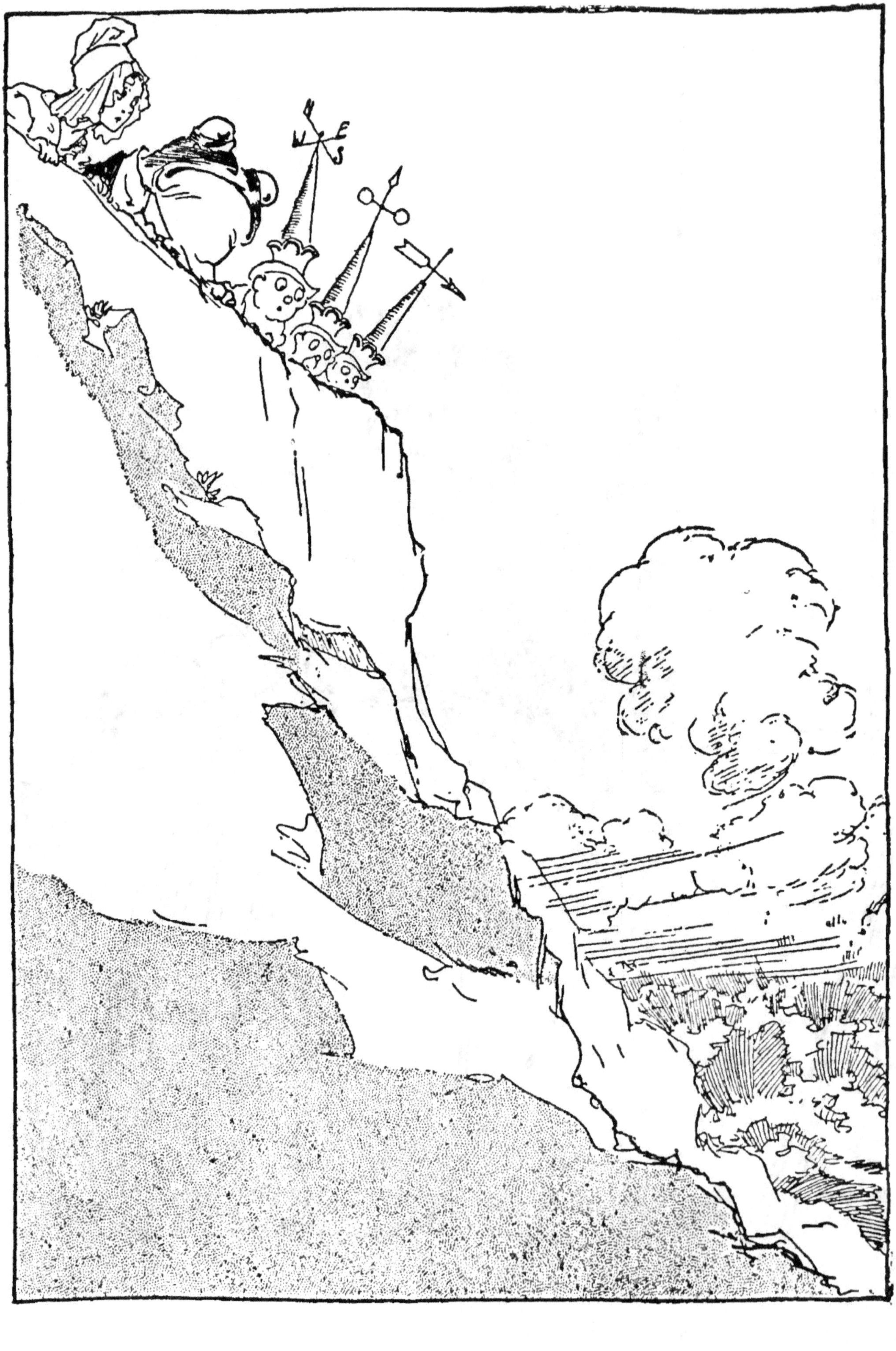
N
W
E
S

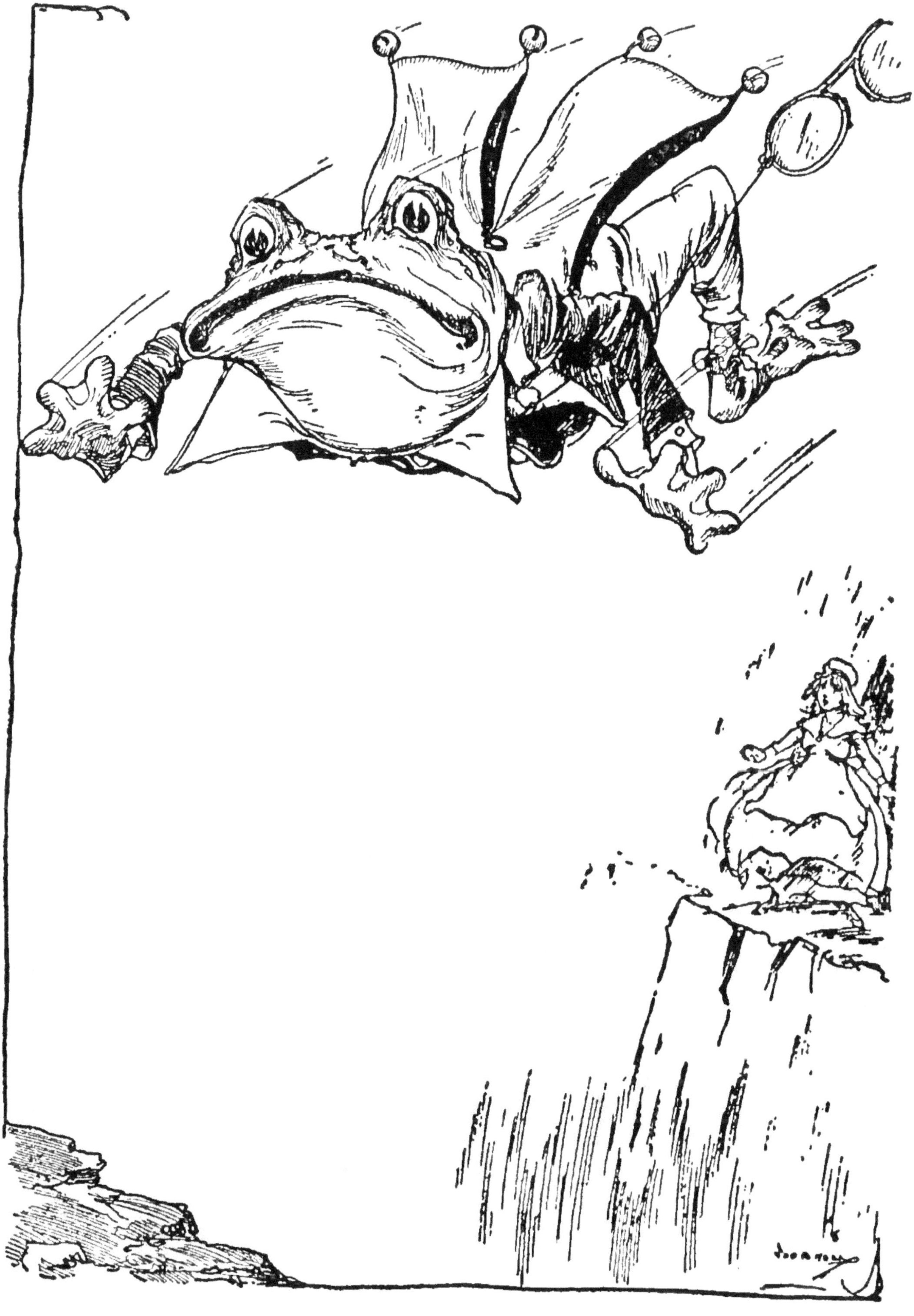

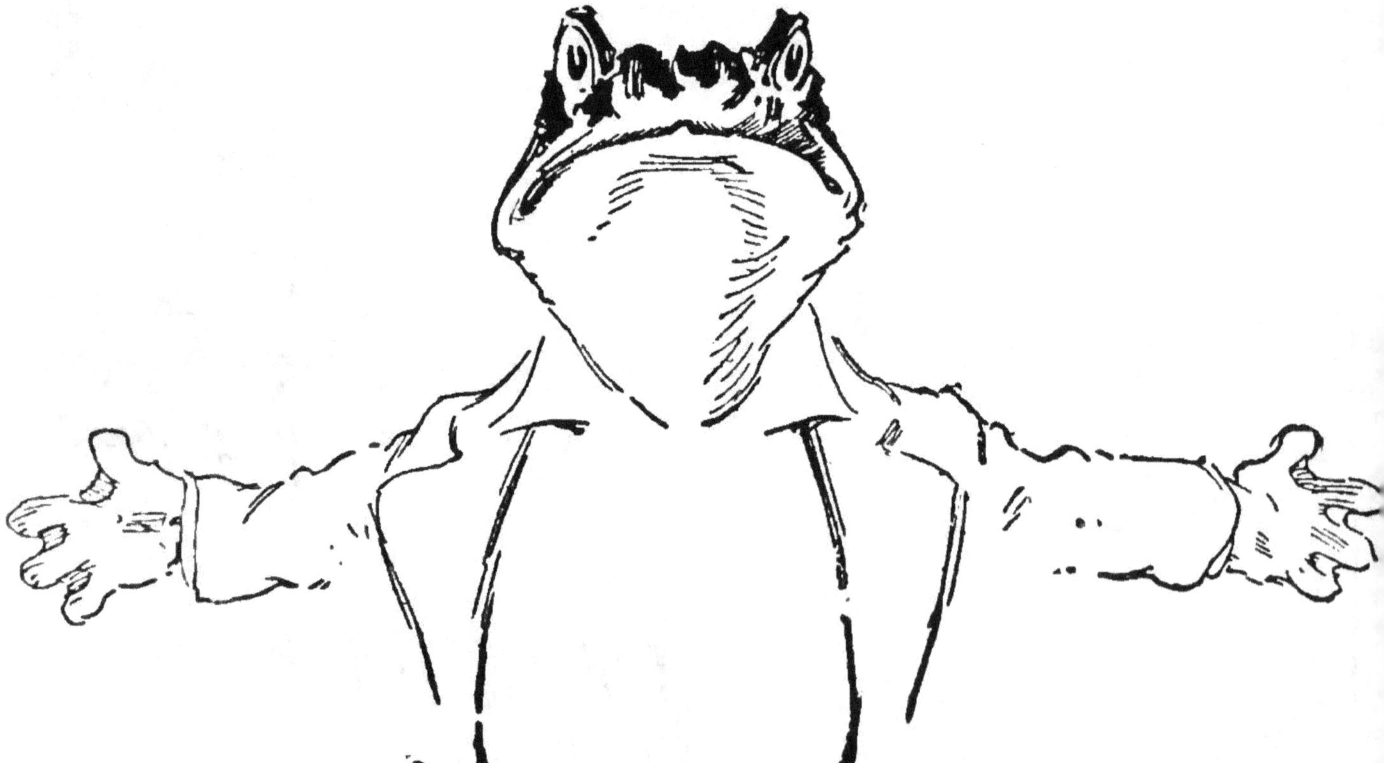

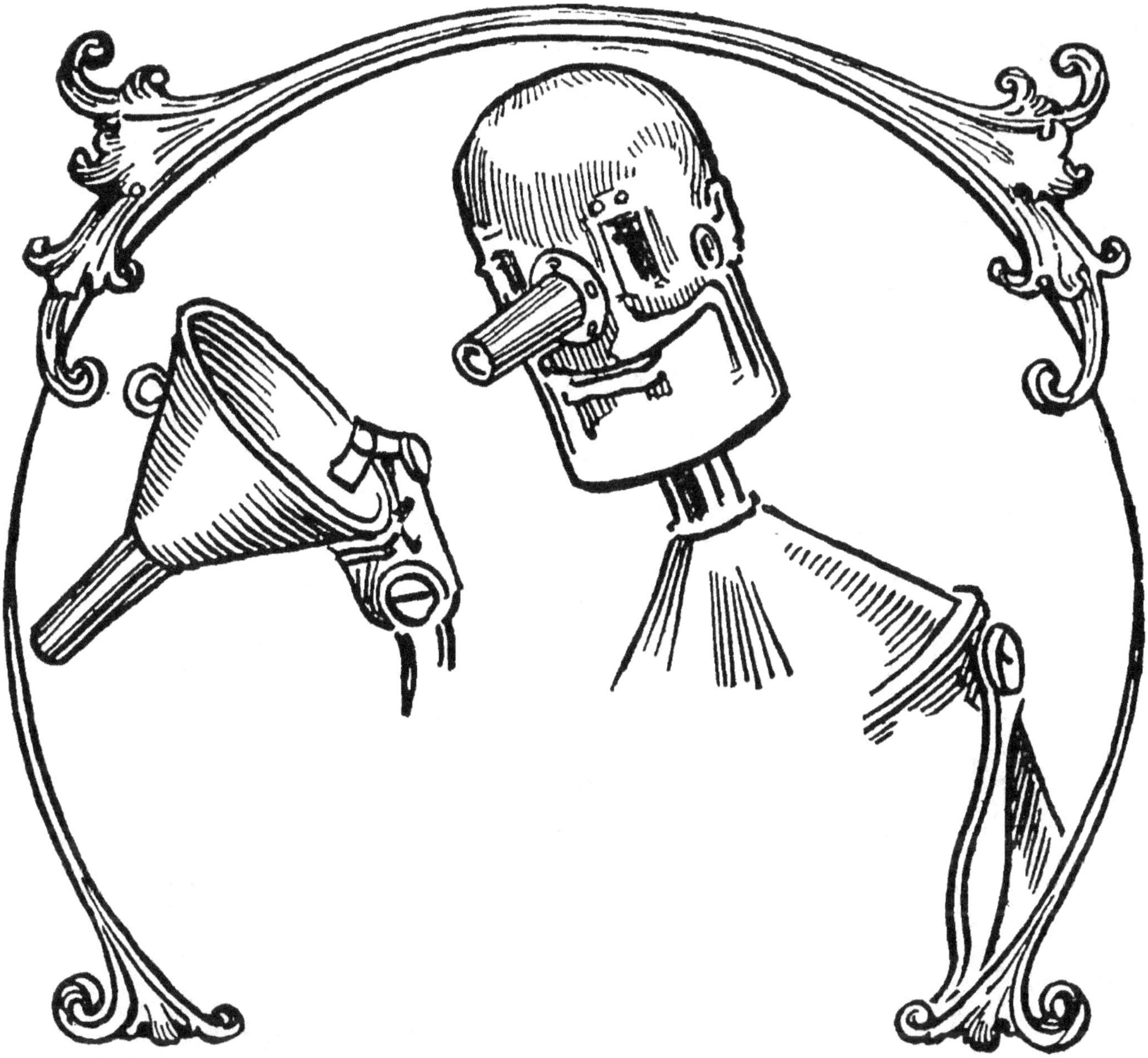

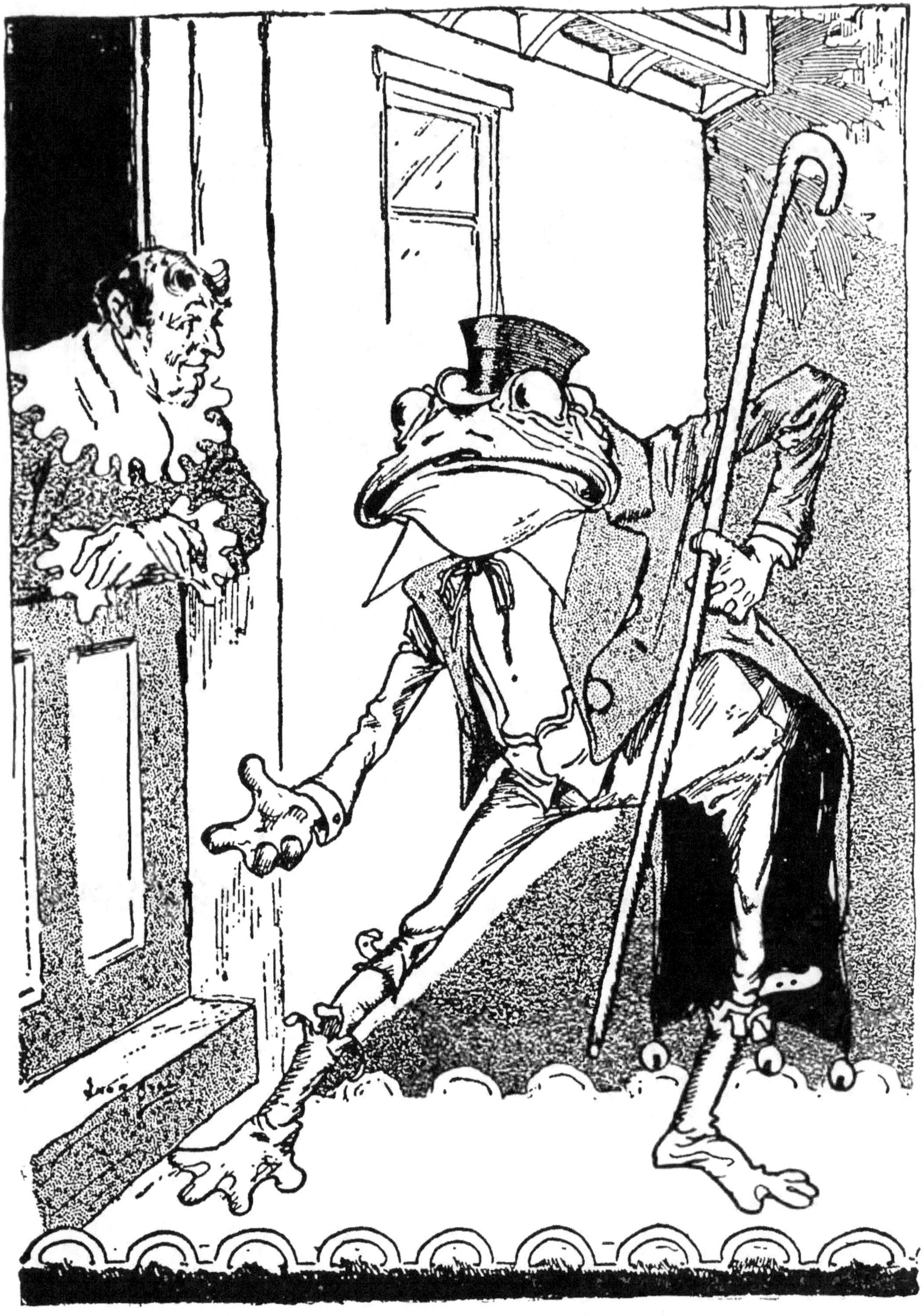

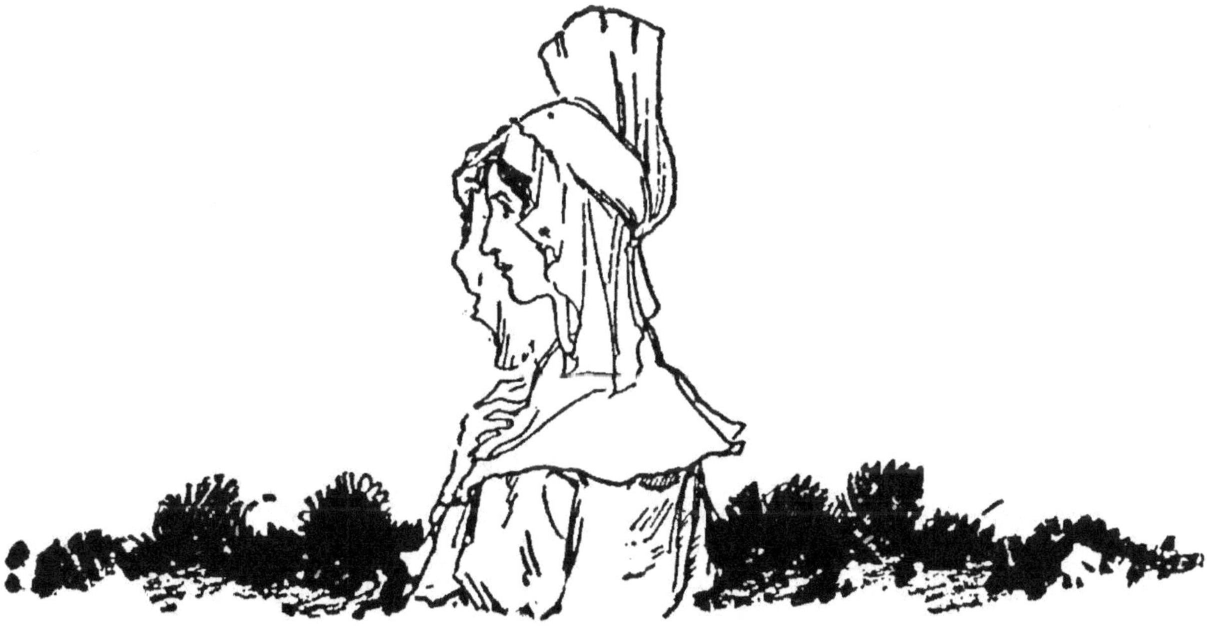

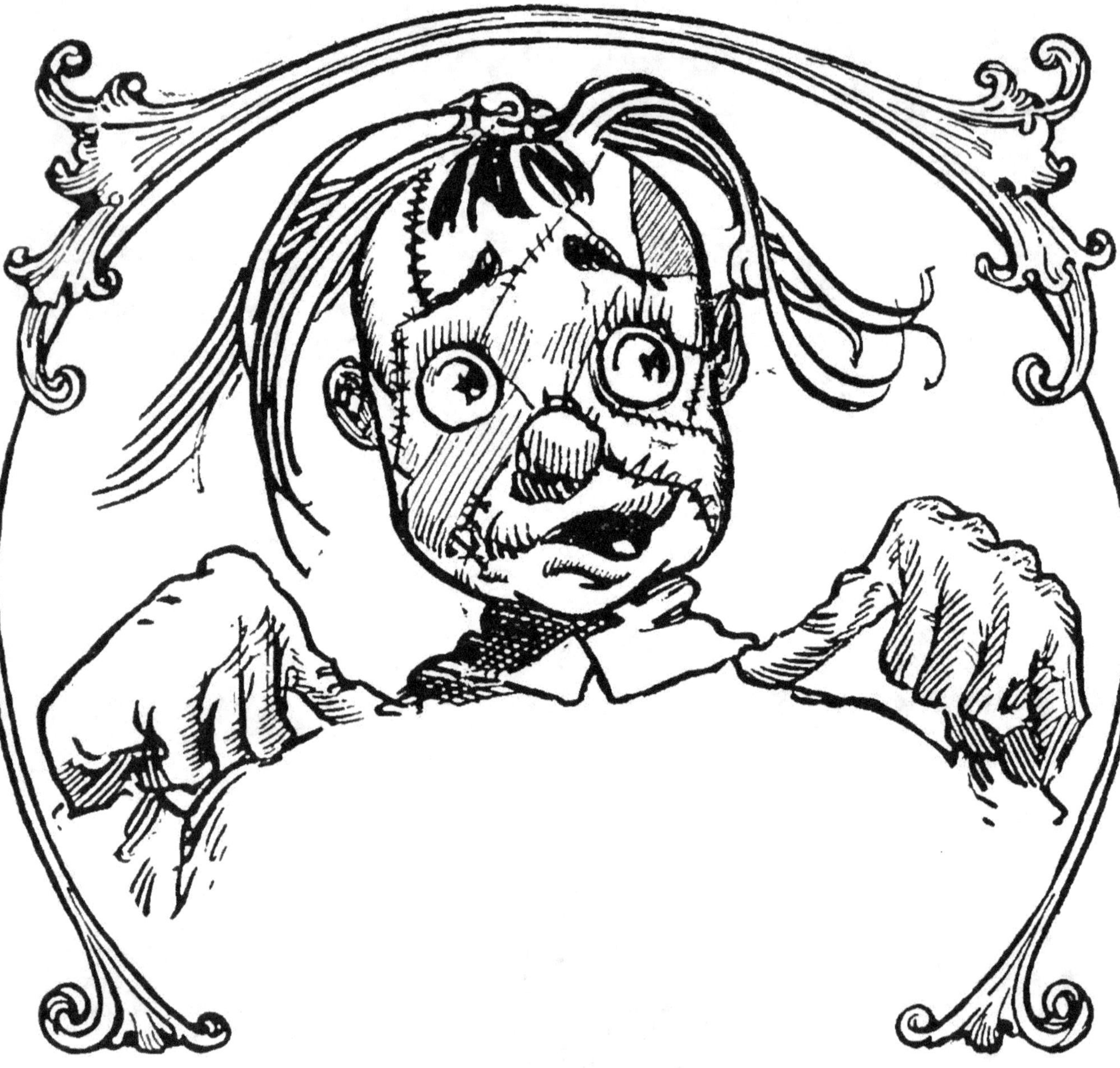

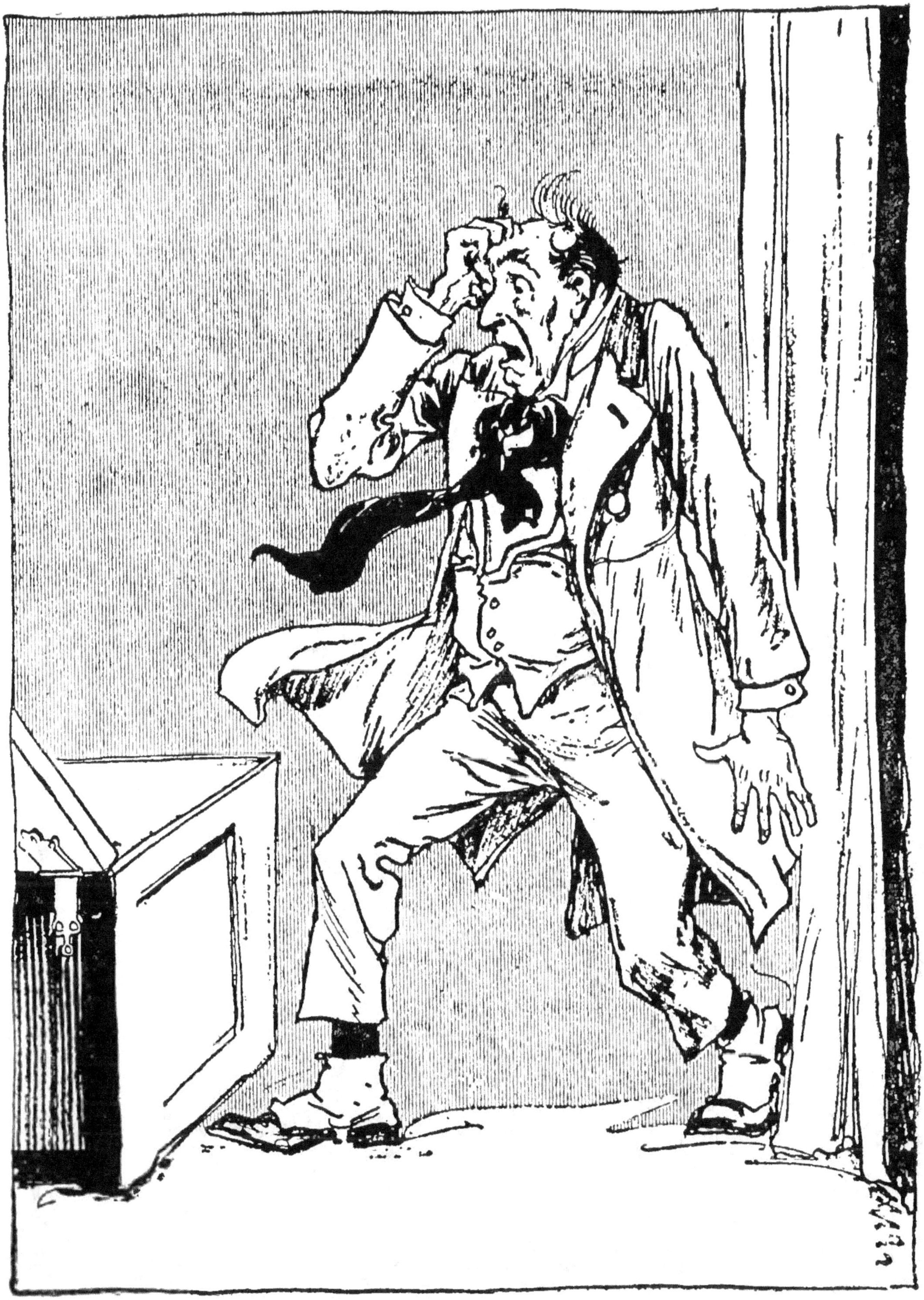

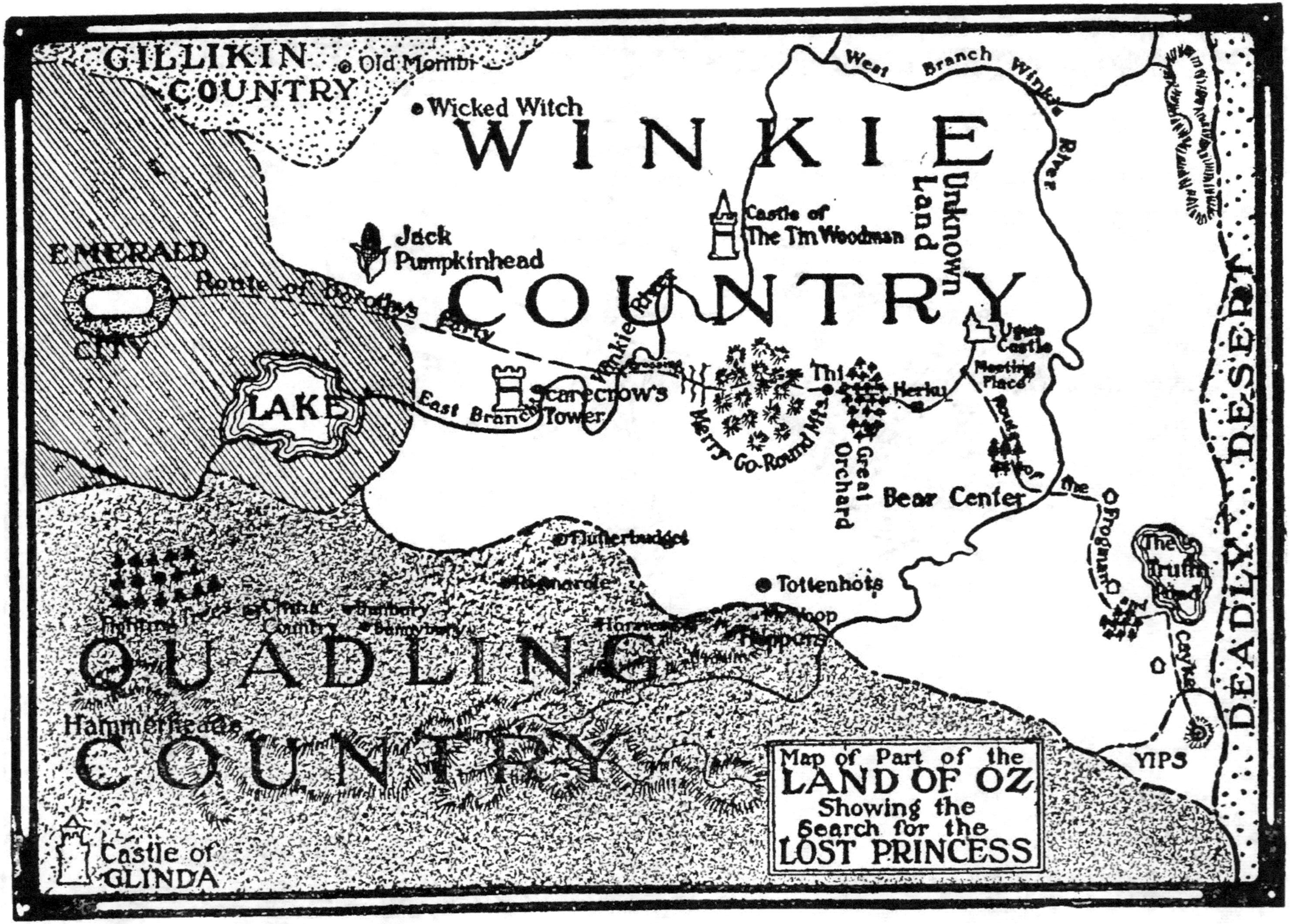
GILLIKIN COUNTRY
Old Mombi
Wicked Witch
WINKIE COUNTRY
Jack Pumpkinhead
EMERALD CITY
Route of Dorothy's Party
Castle of The Tin Woodman
Unknown Land
West Branch Winkie River
Winkie River
LAKE
East Branch
Scarecrow's Tower
Merry-Go-Round Mts.
Thi
Herku
Great Orchard
Ugu's Castle
Meeting Place
Bear Center
Frogman
The Truth Pond
Cayke
YIPS
DEADLY DESERT
Flutterbudget
Tottenhots
Herku
Hoppers
QUADLING COUNTRY
Hammerheads
Castle of GLINDA
Map of Part of the LAND OF OZ Showing the Search for the LOST PRINCESS

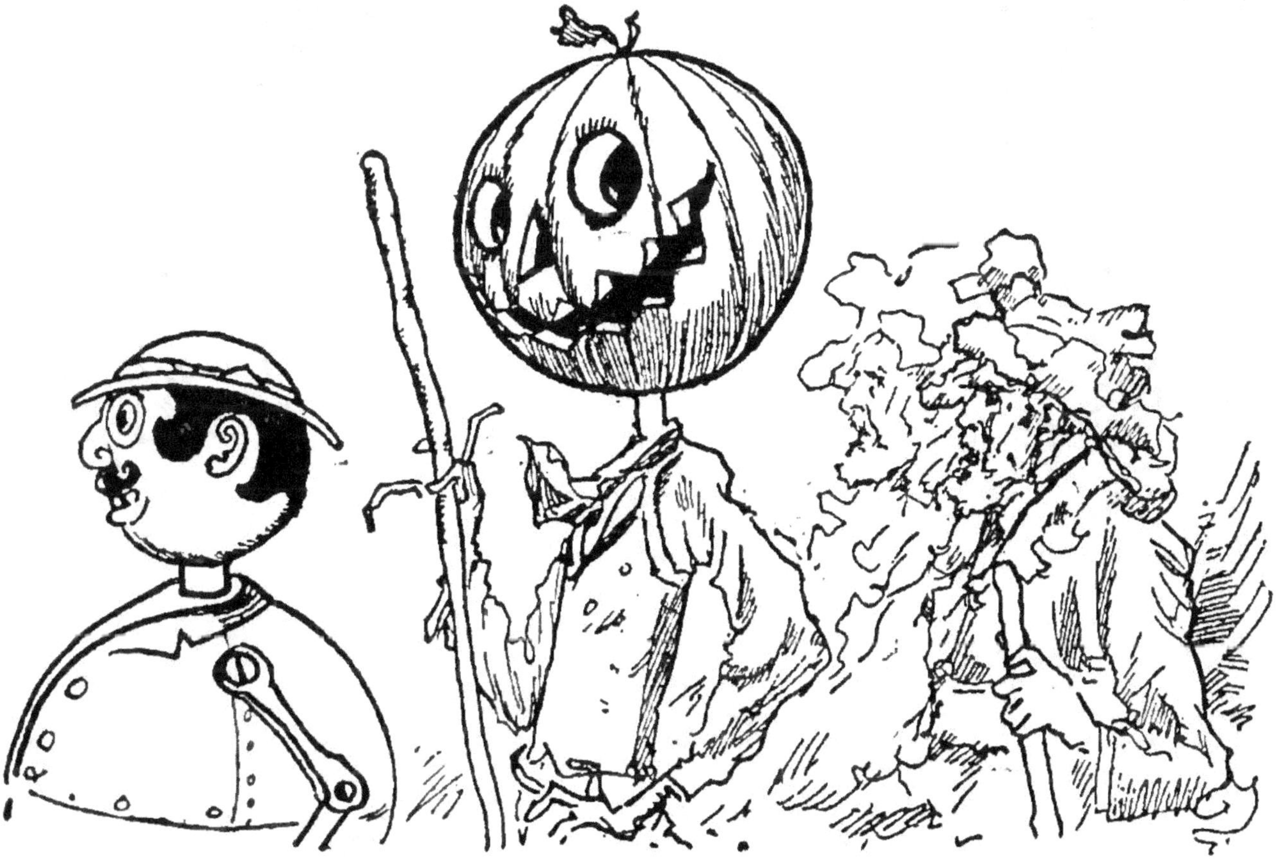

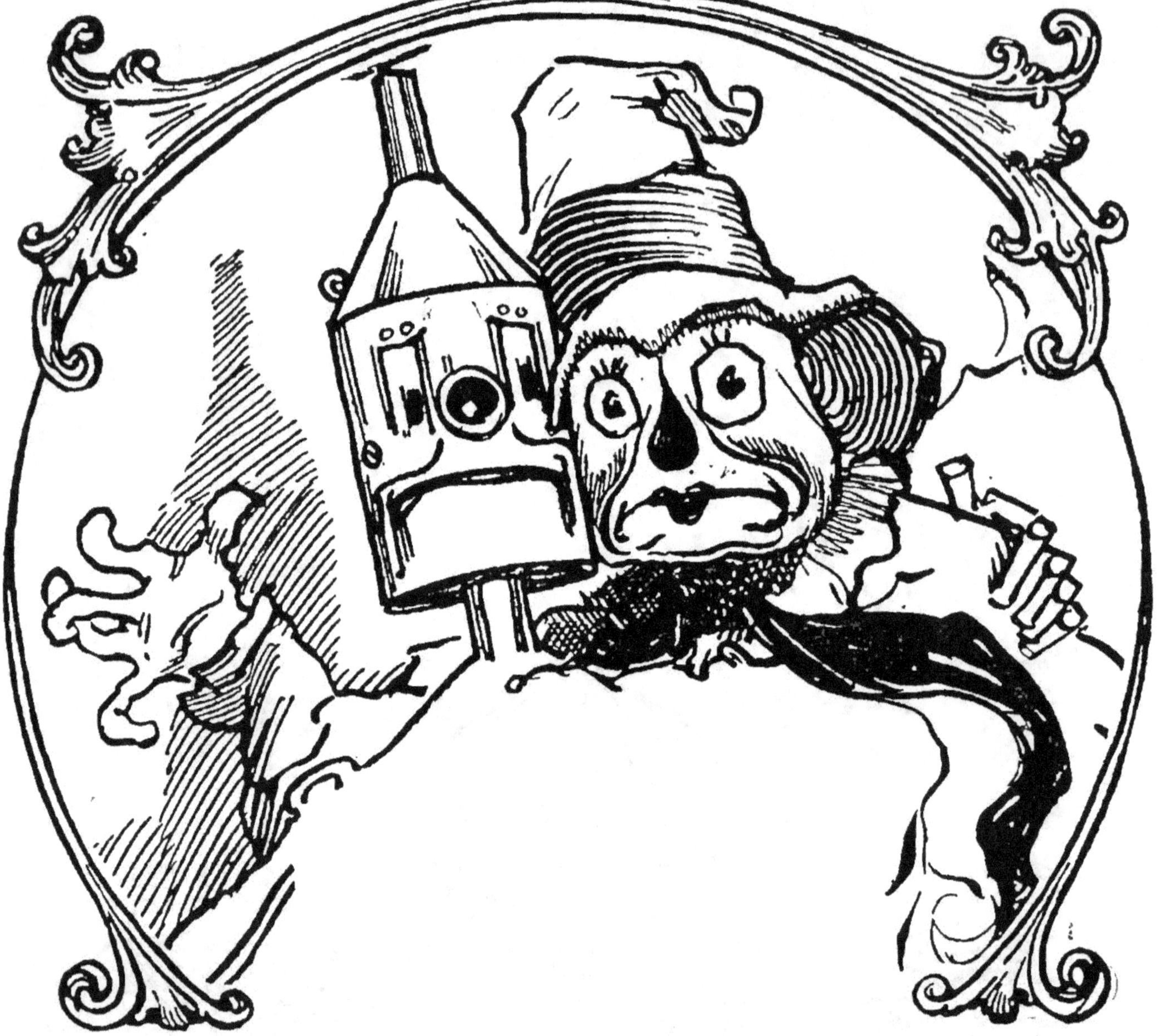

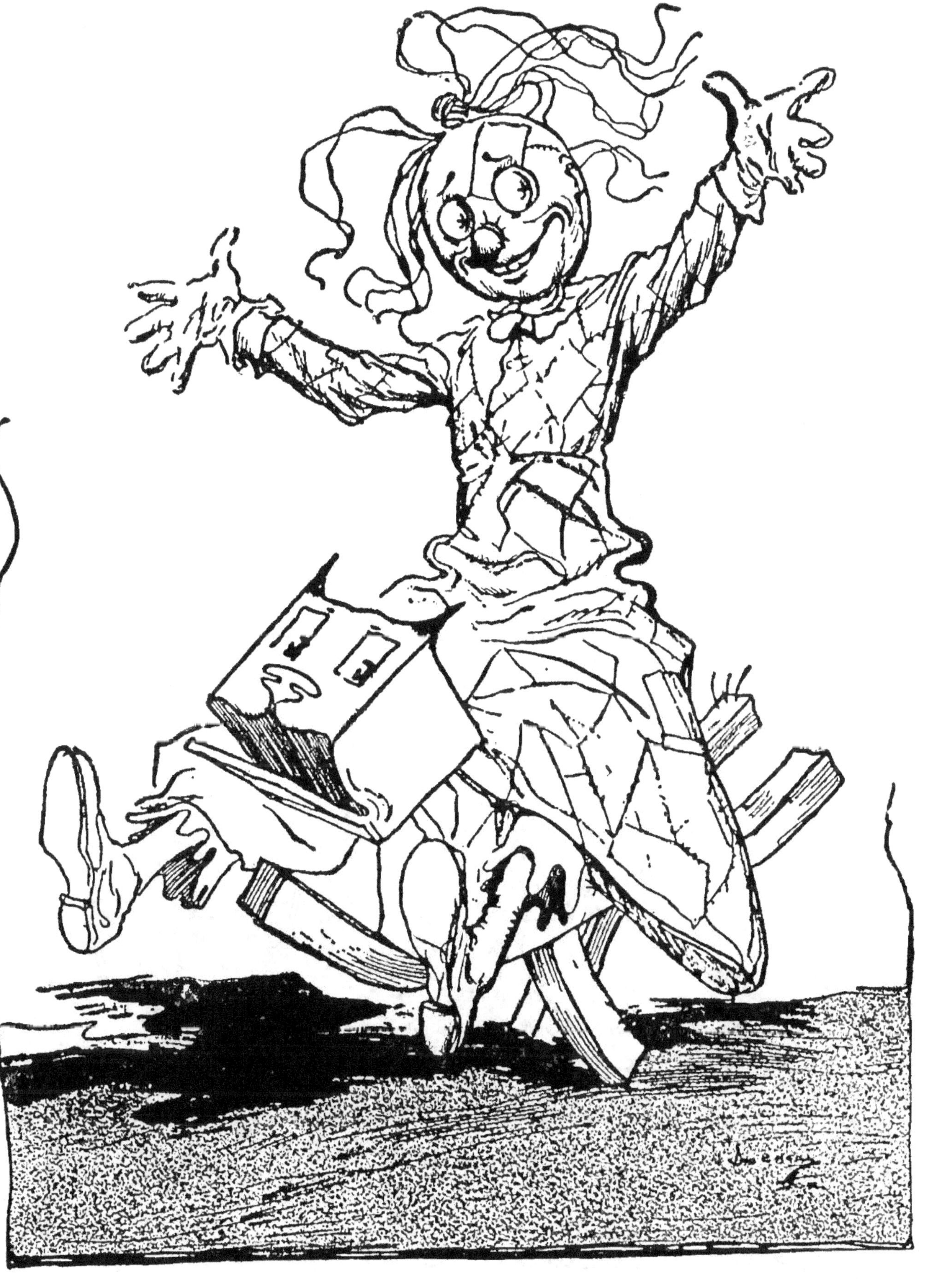

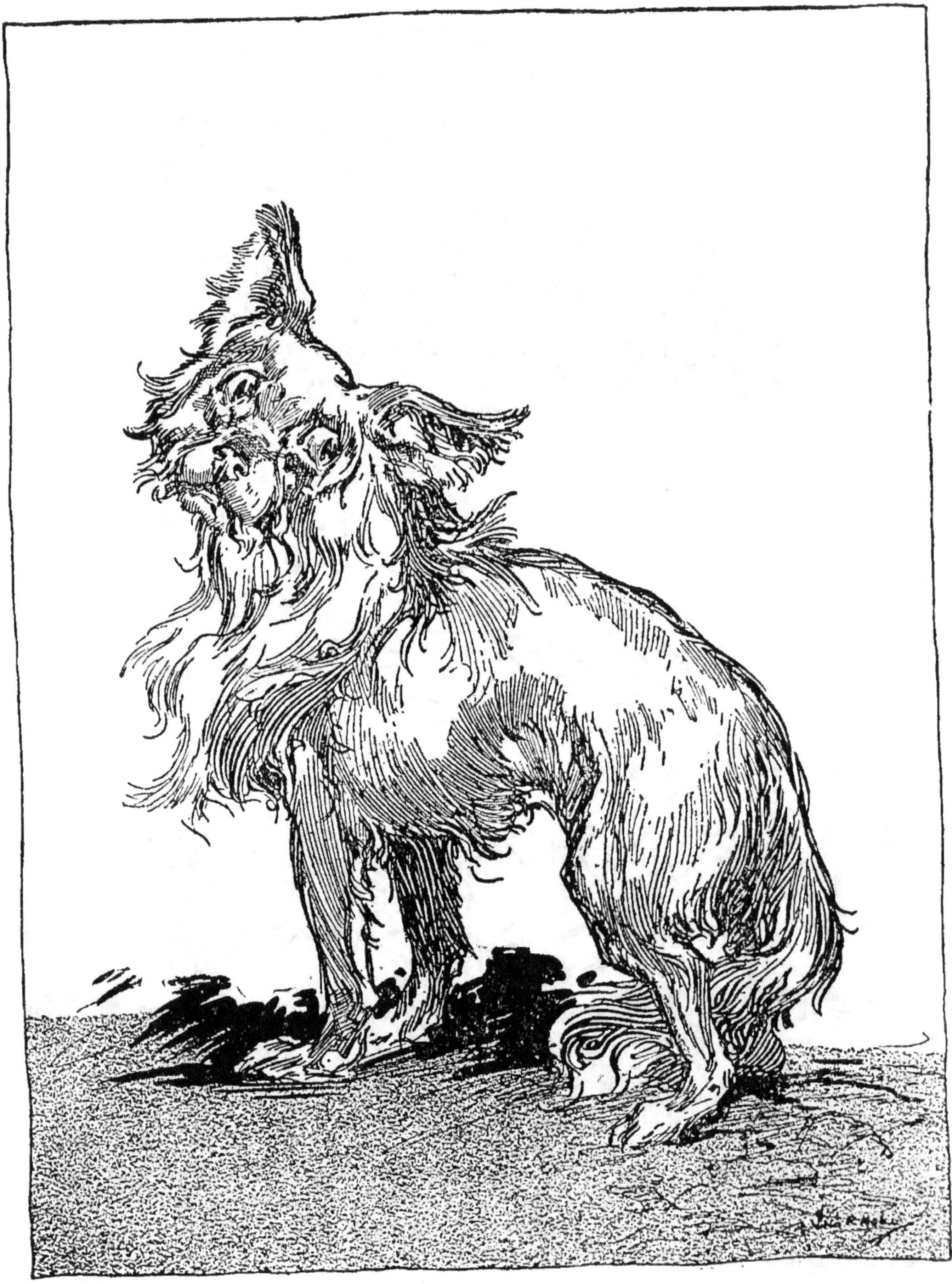

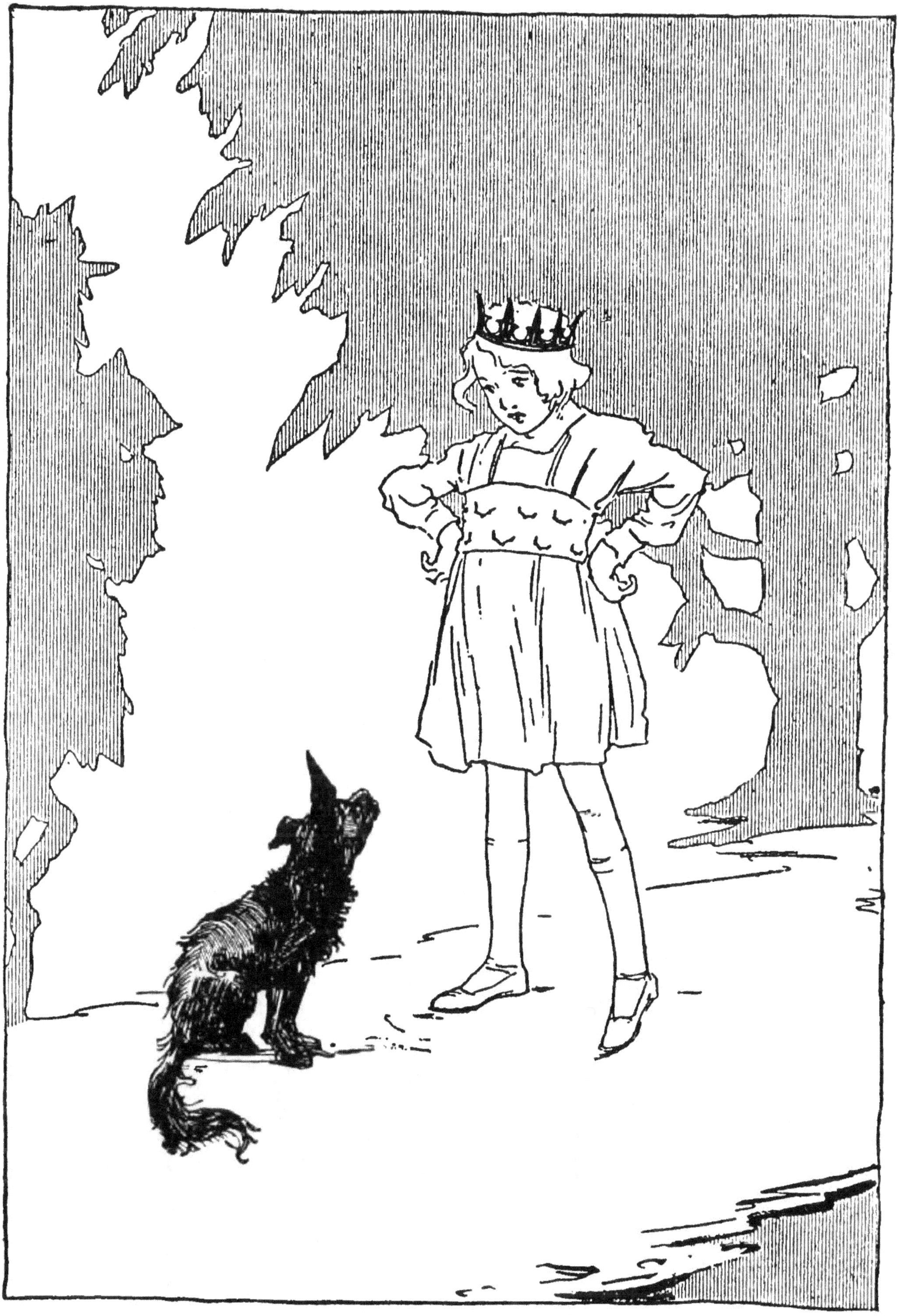

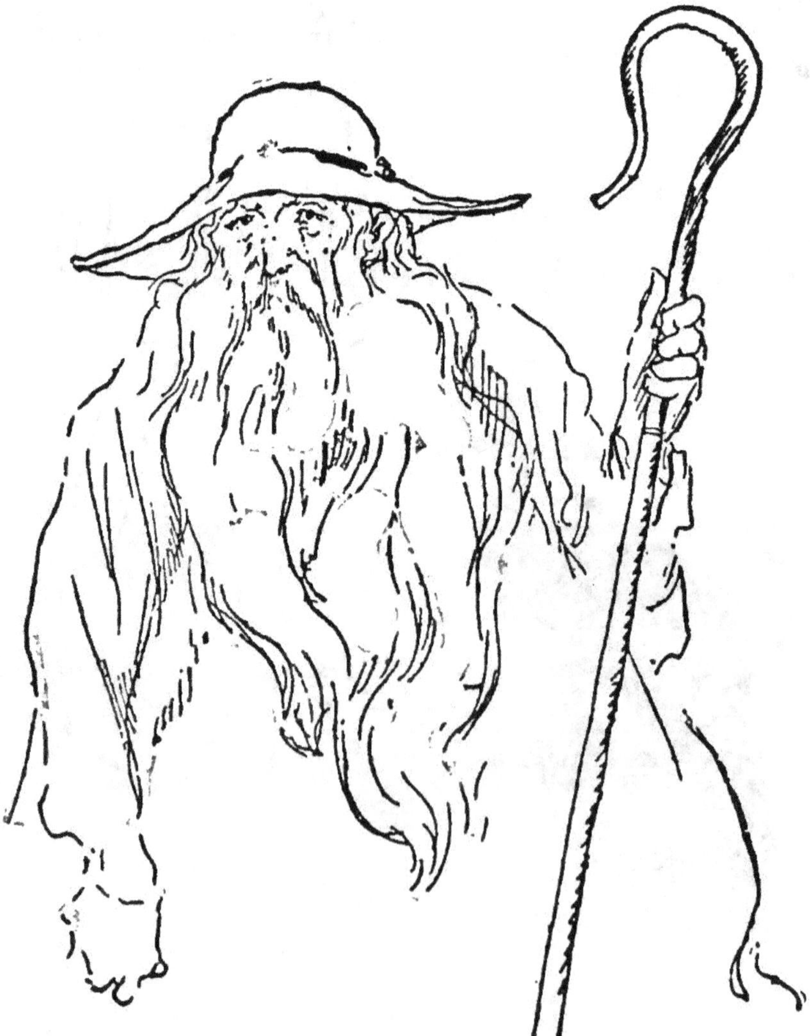

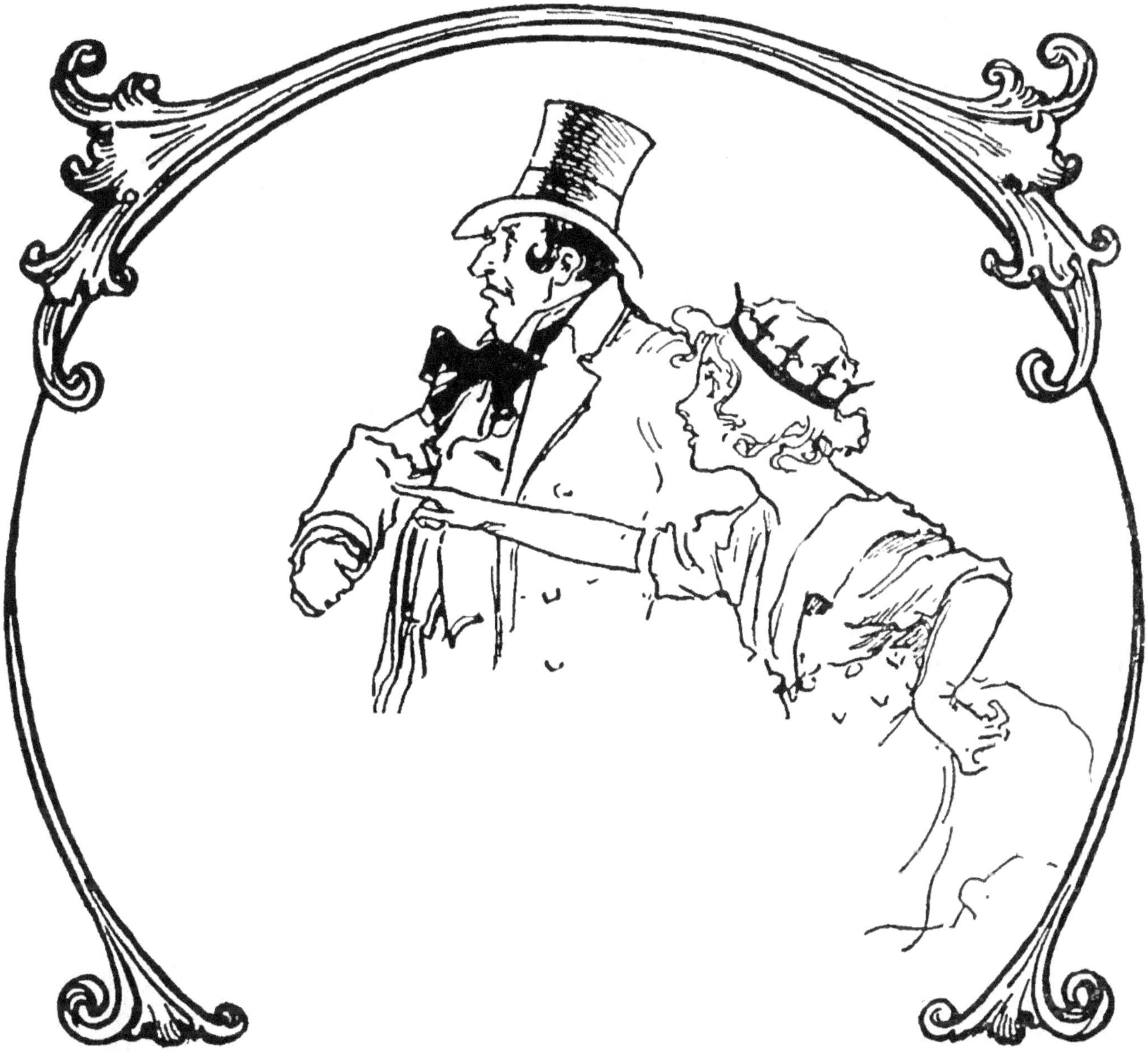

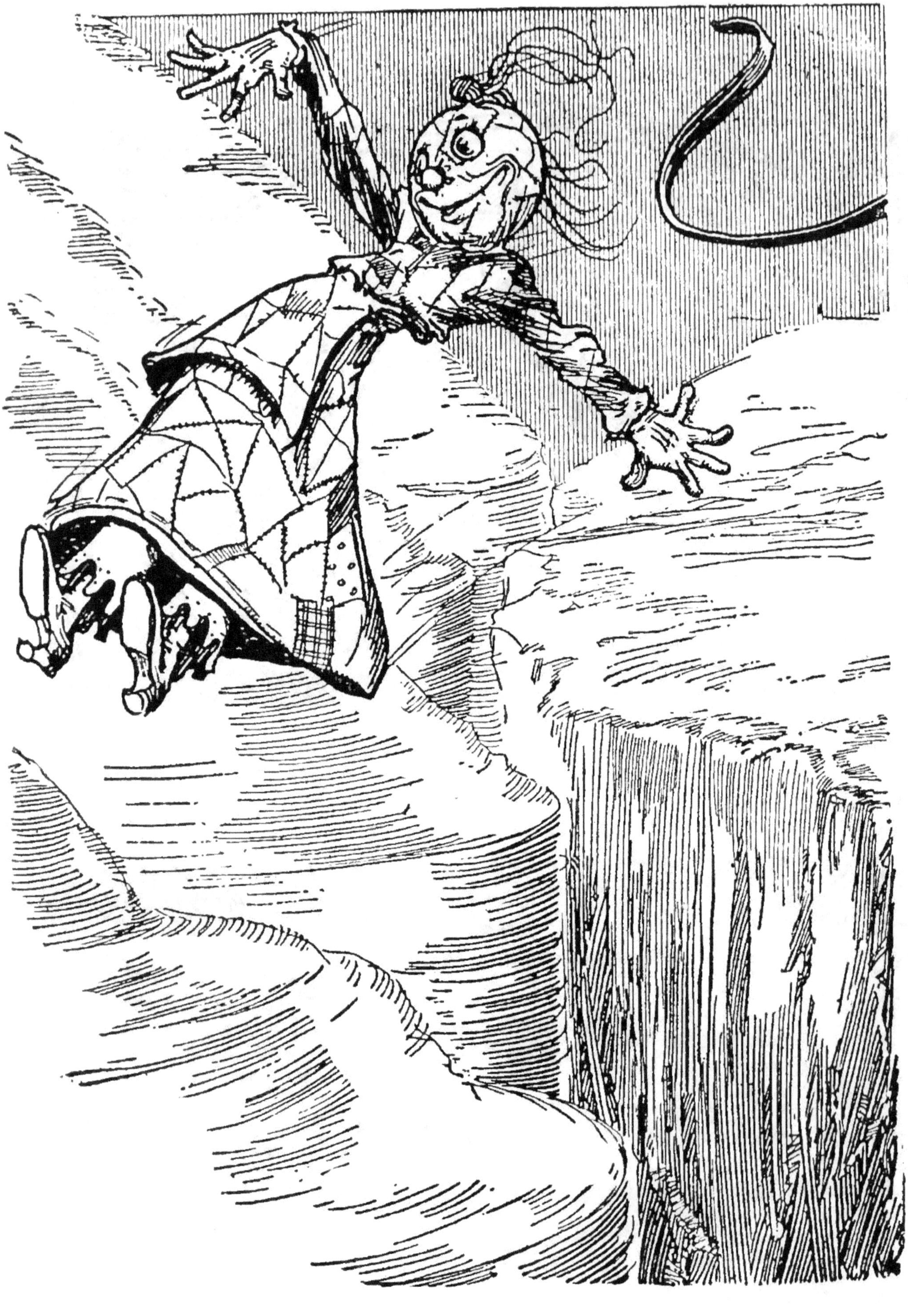

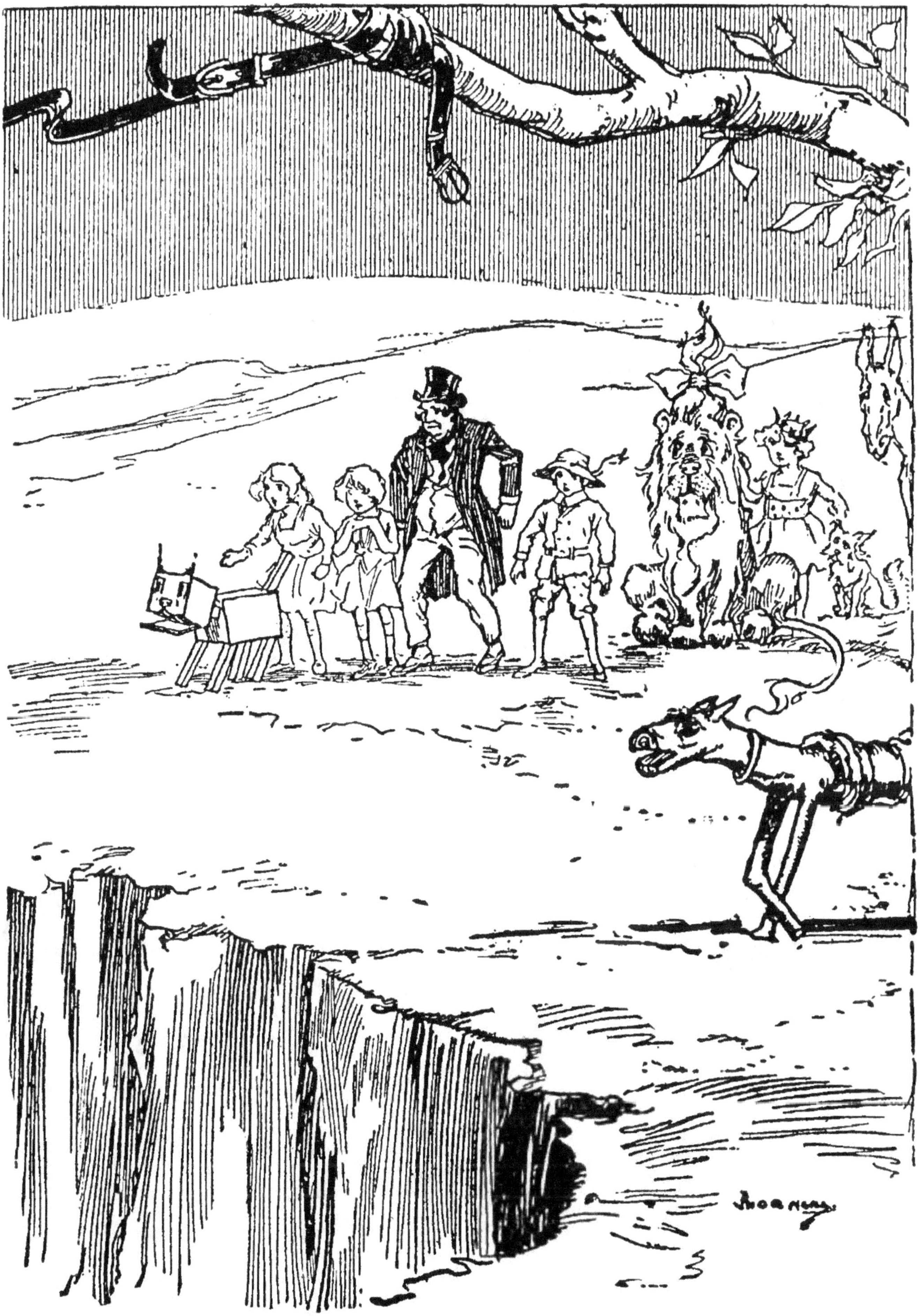

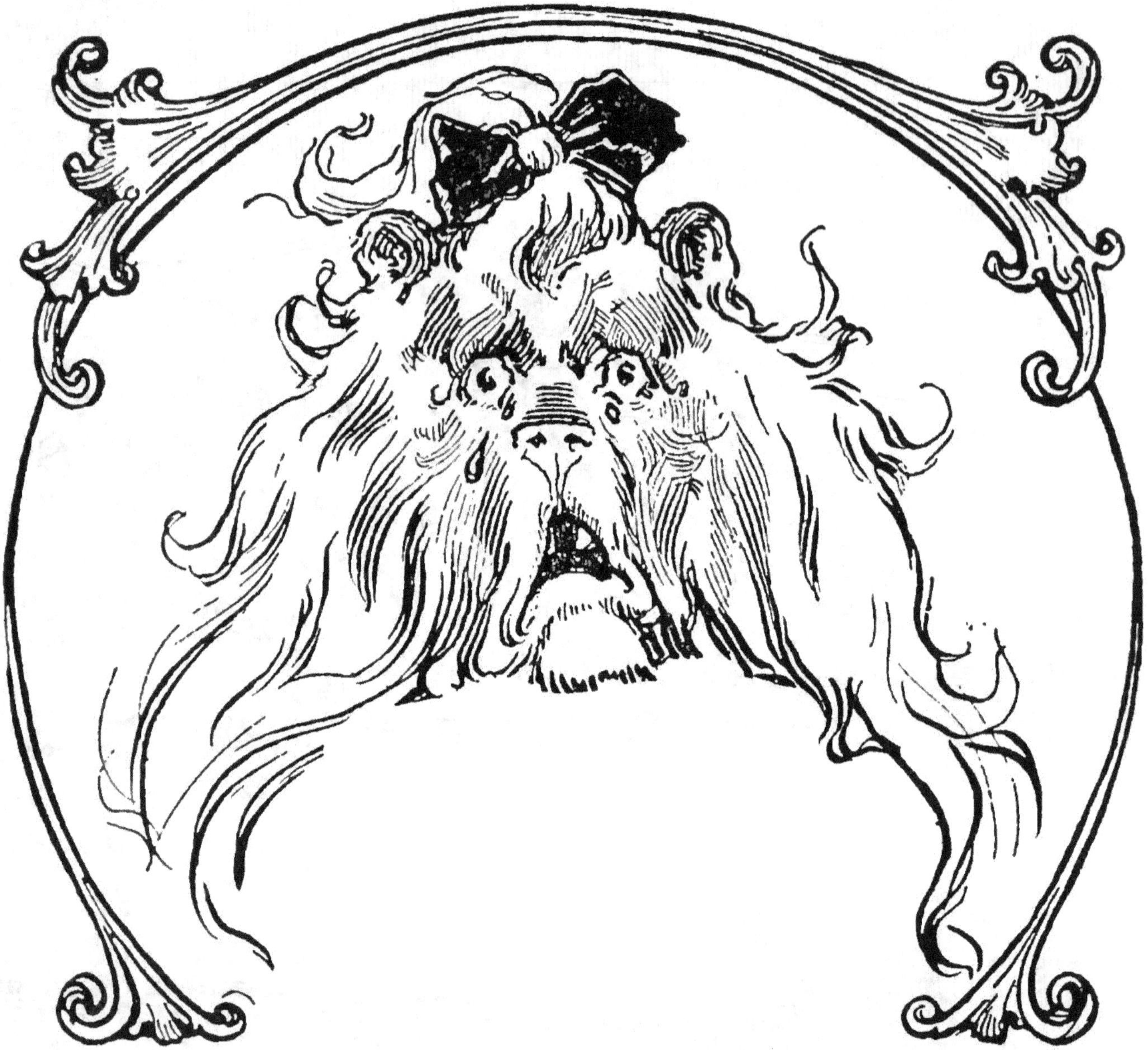

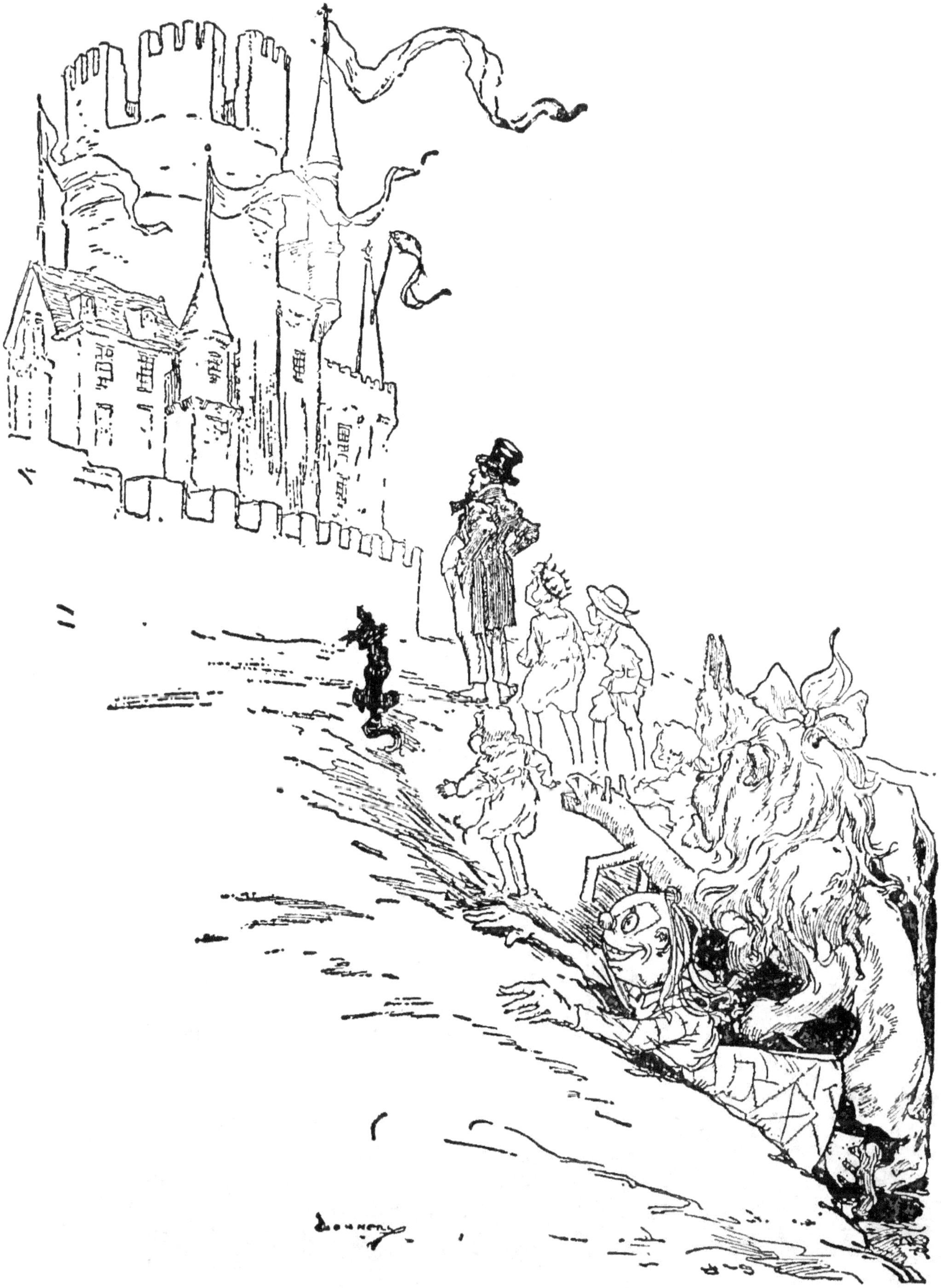

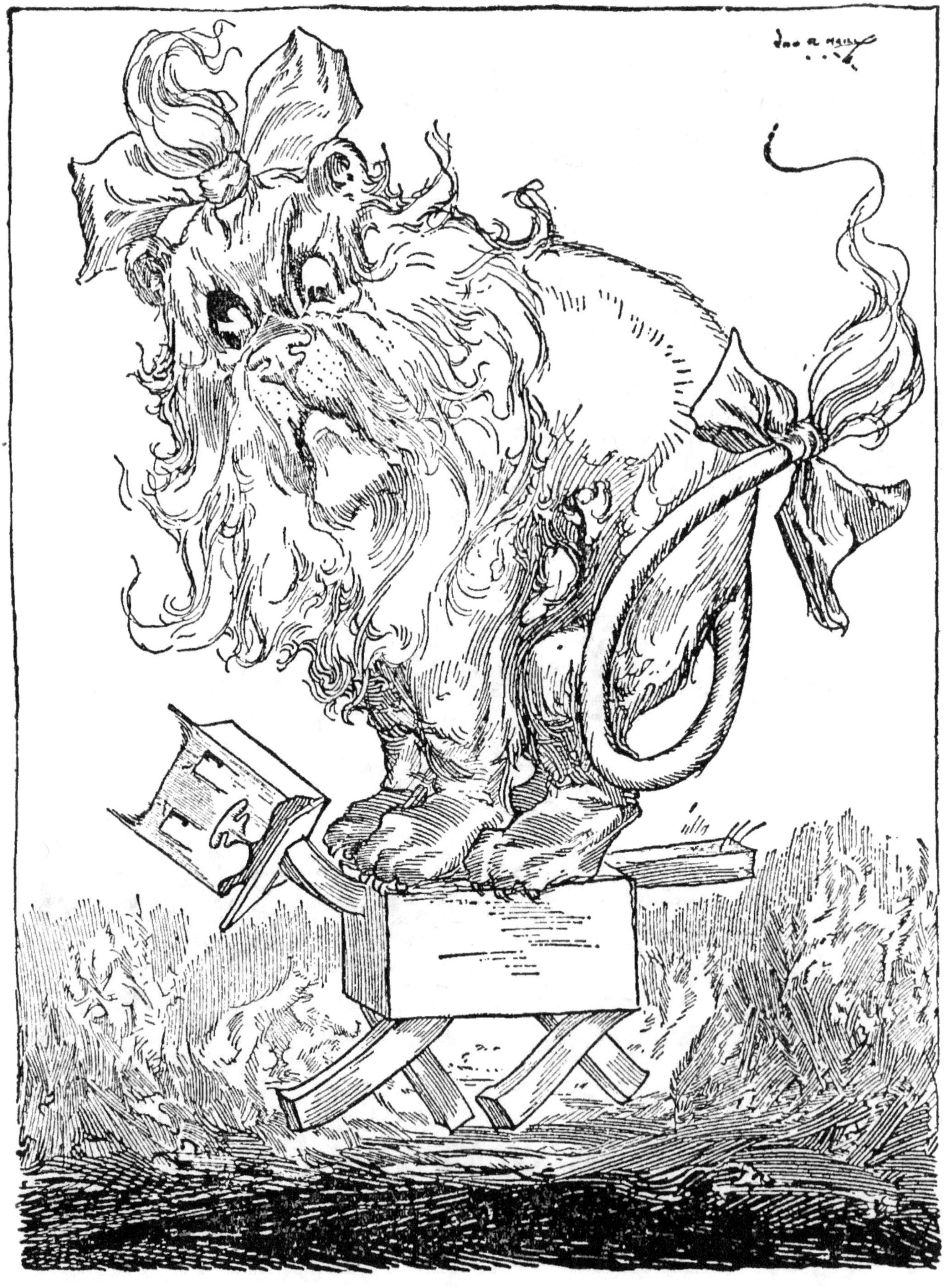

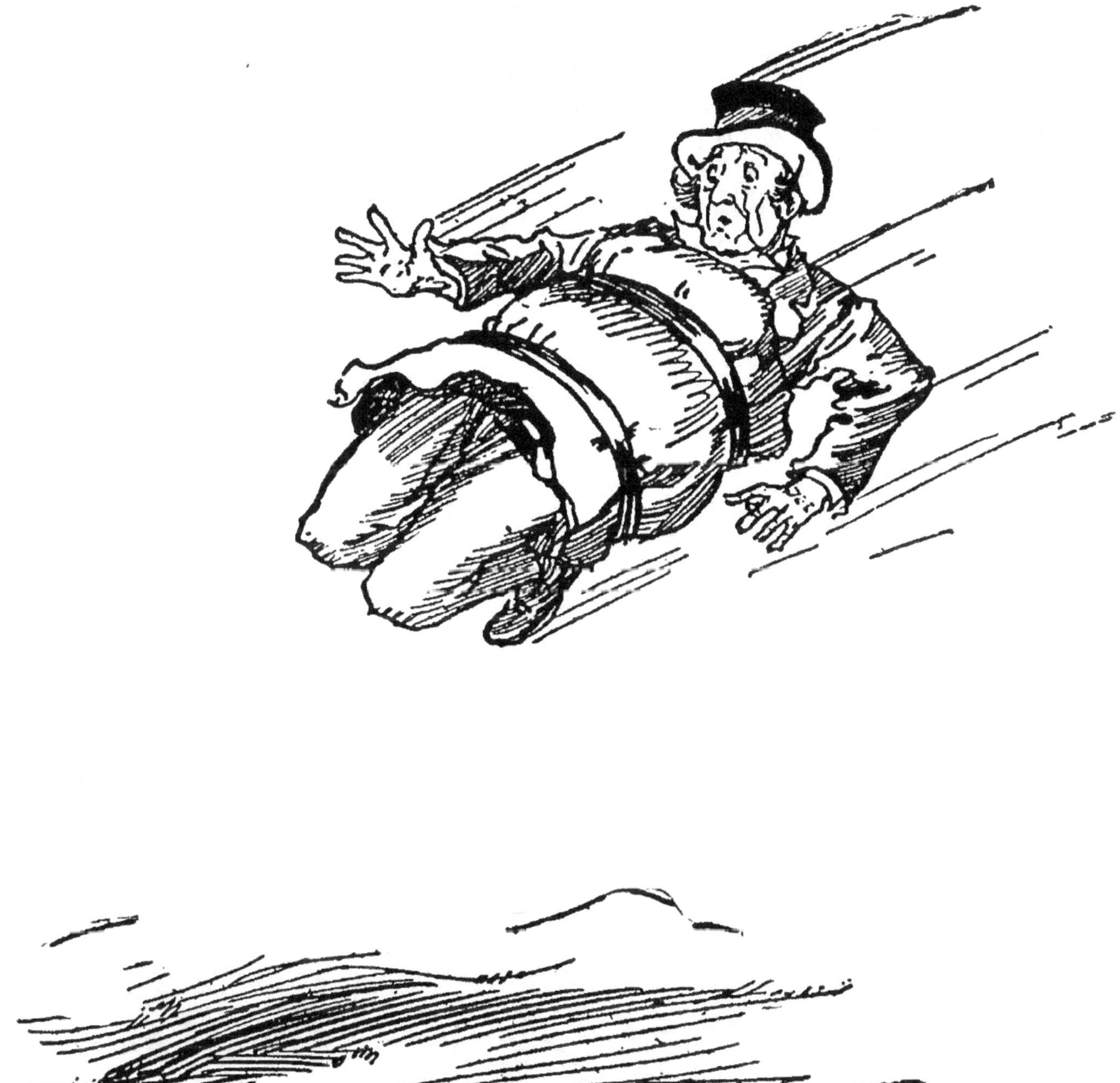

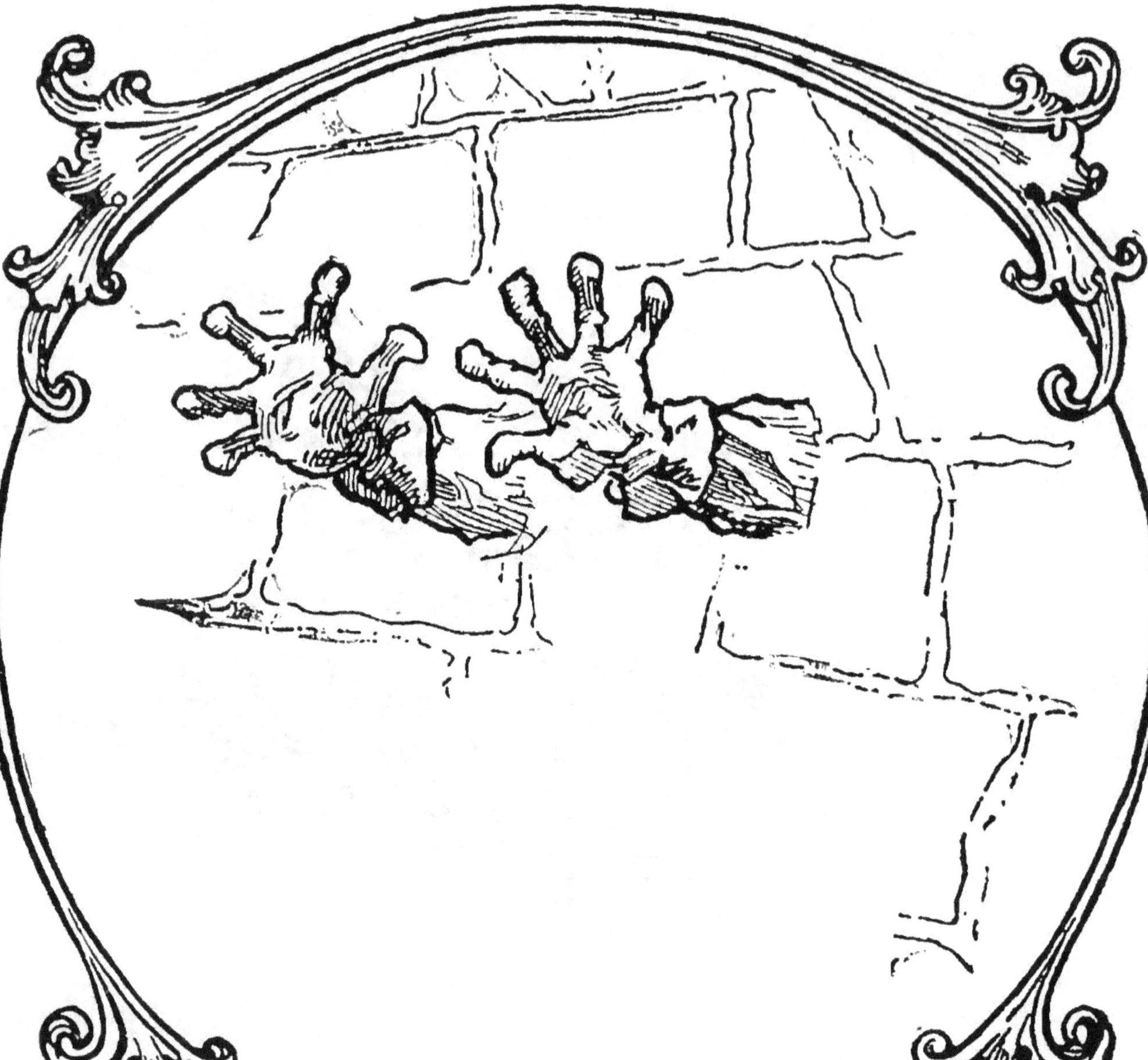

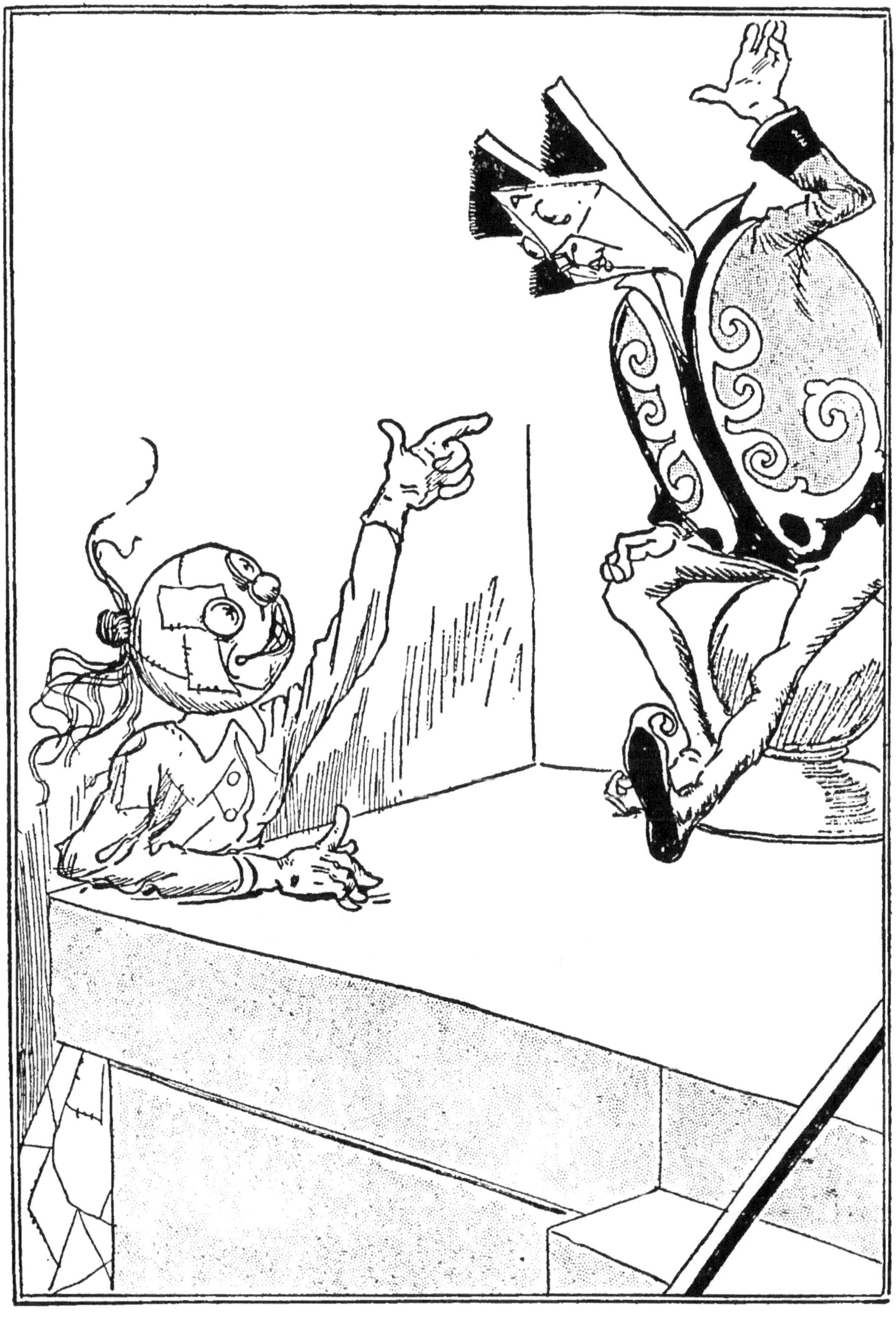

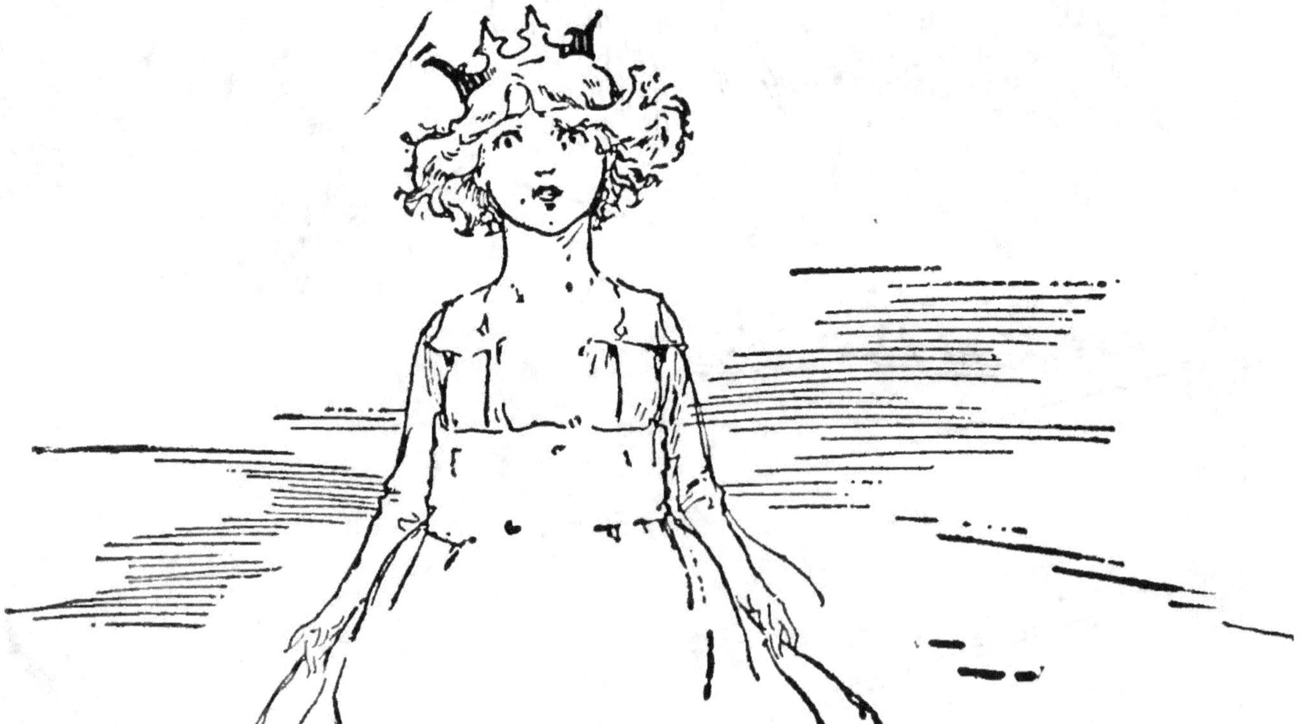

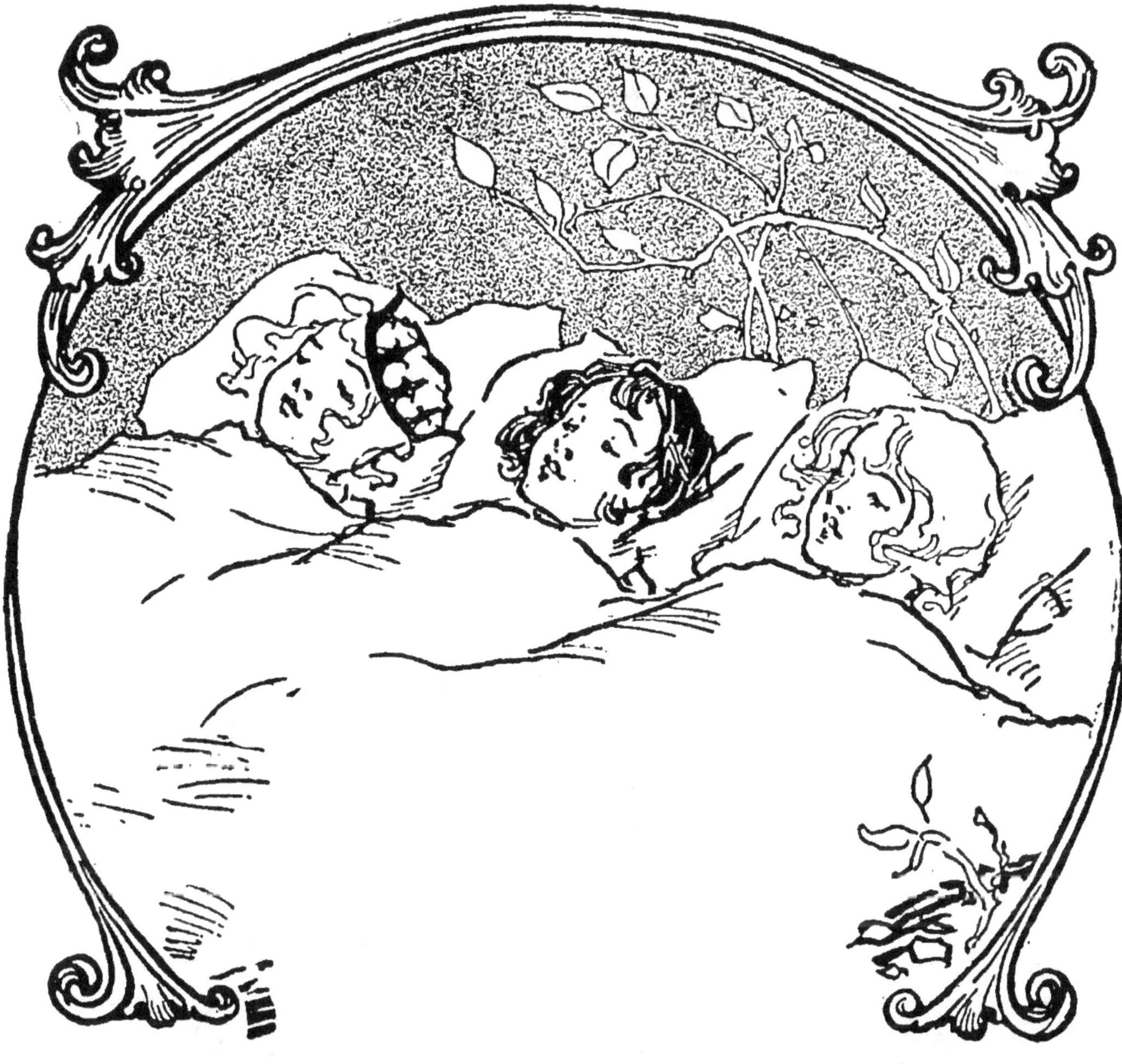

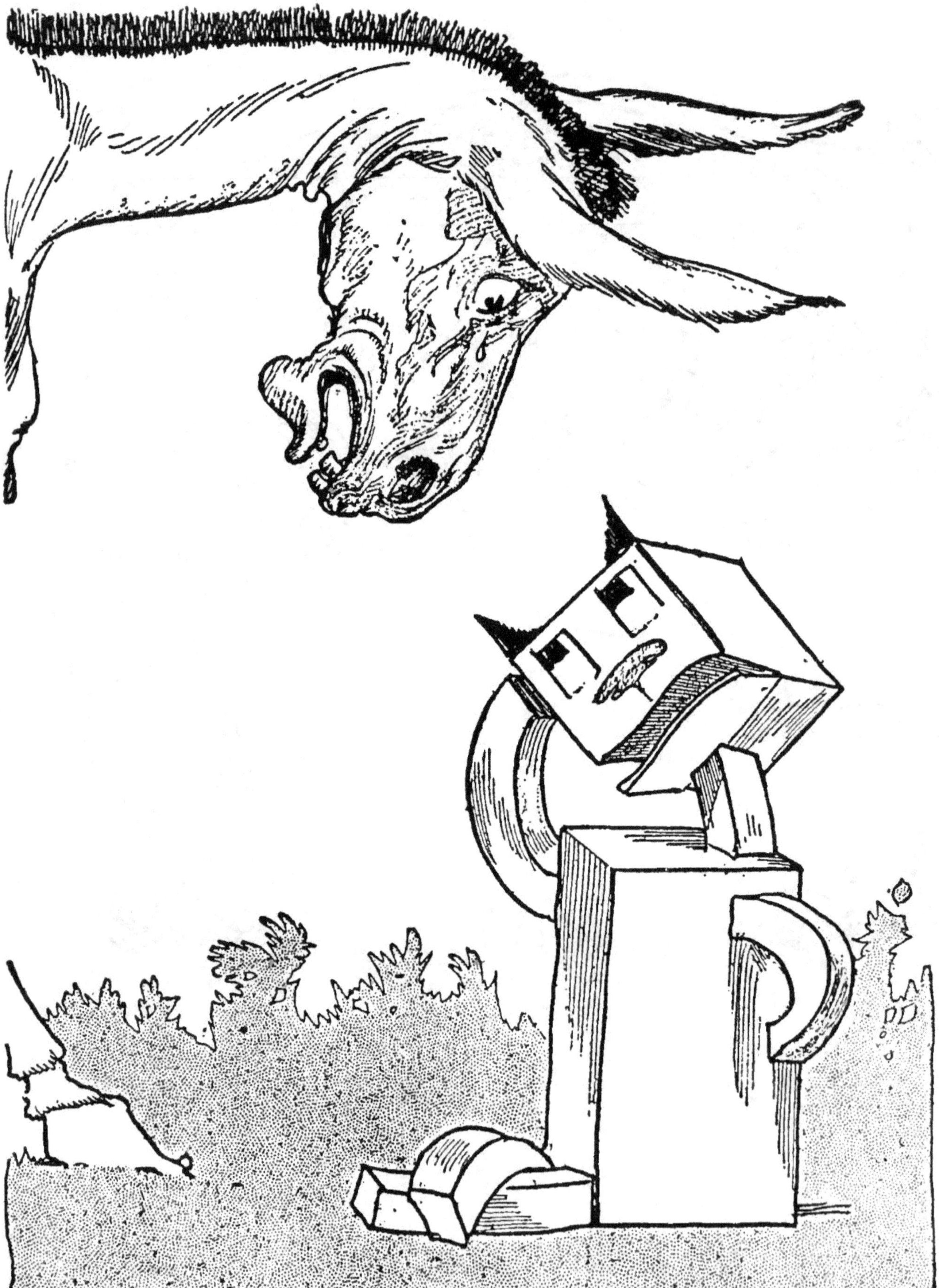

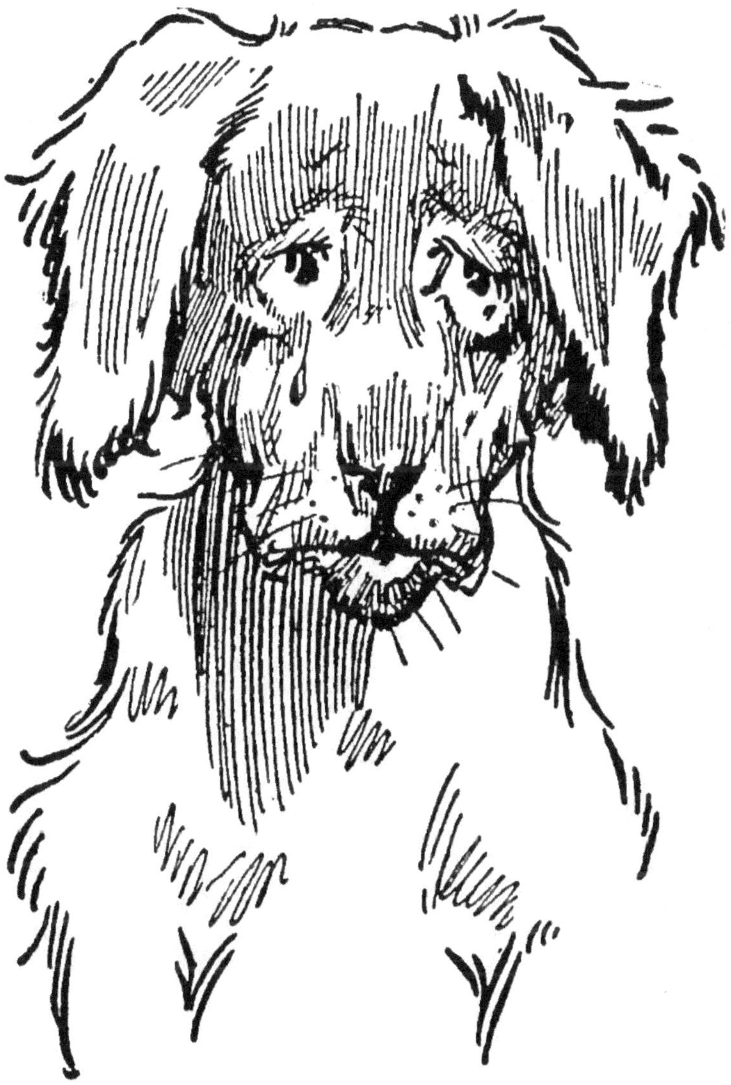

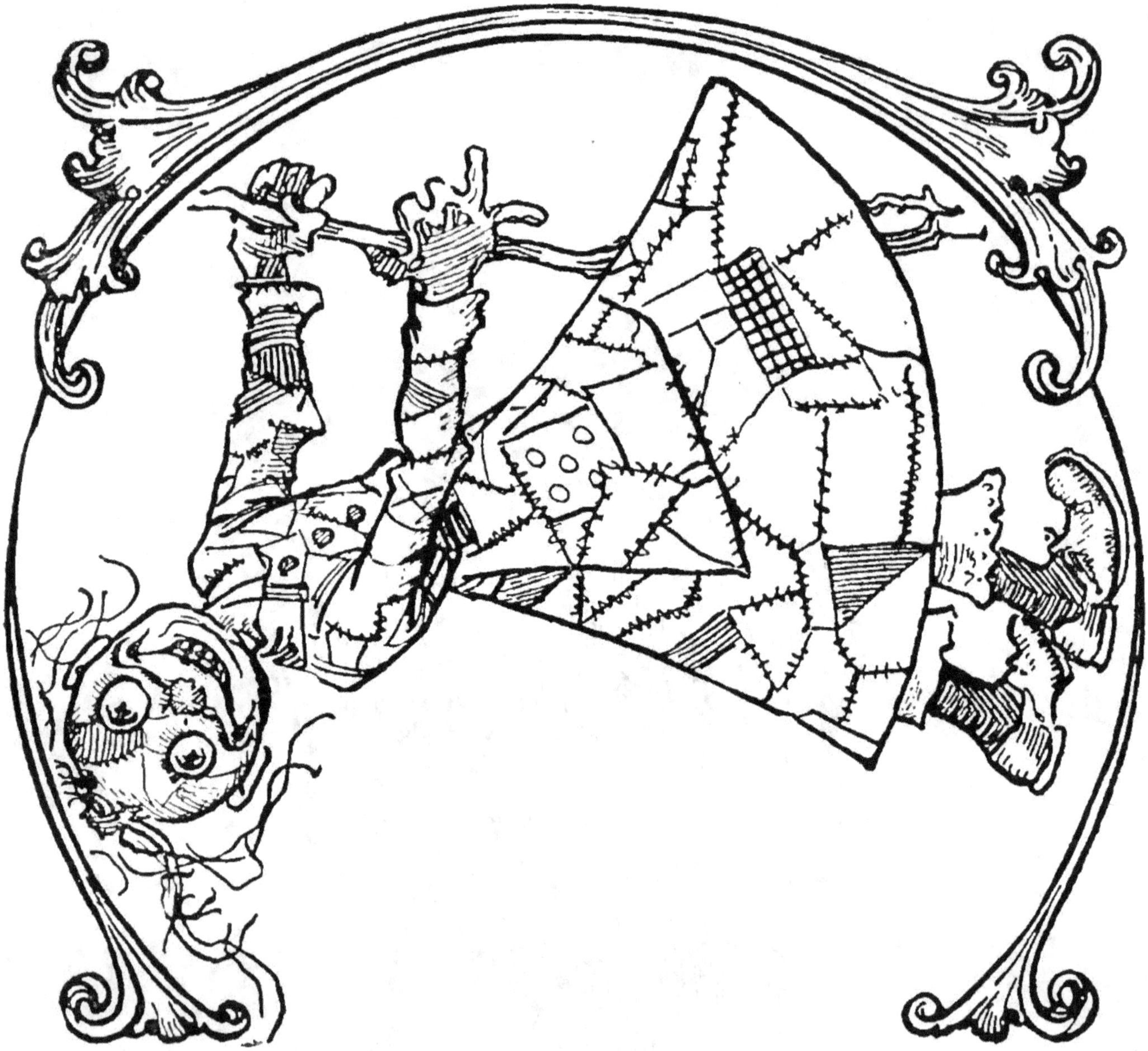

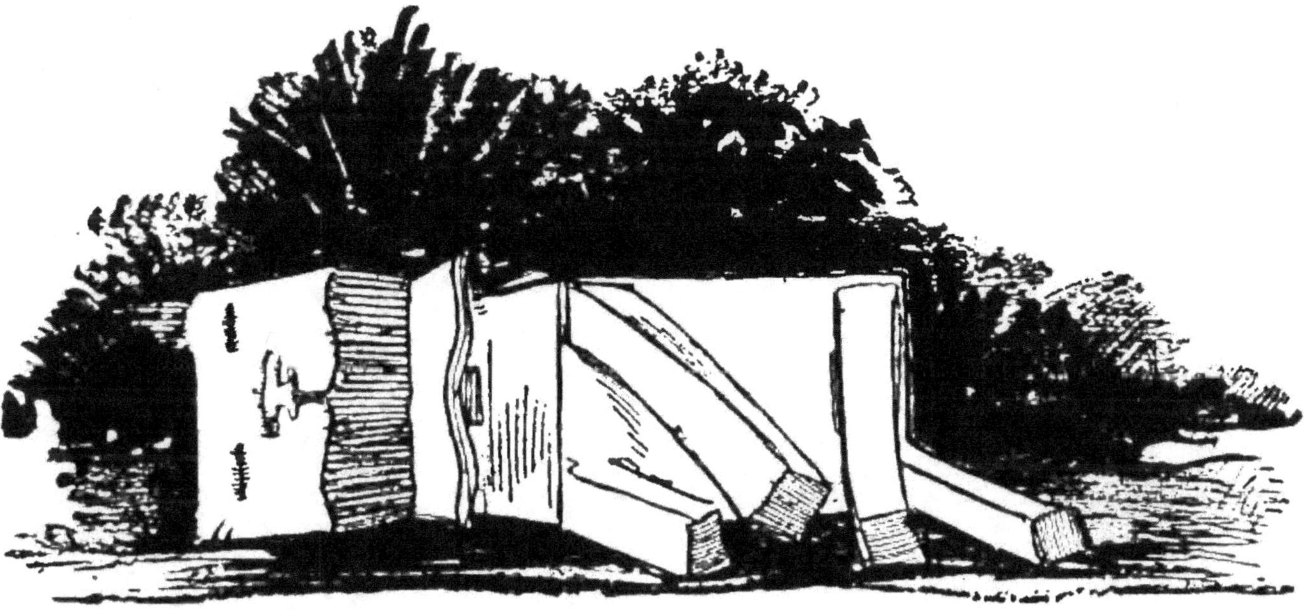

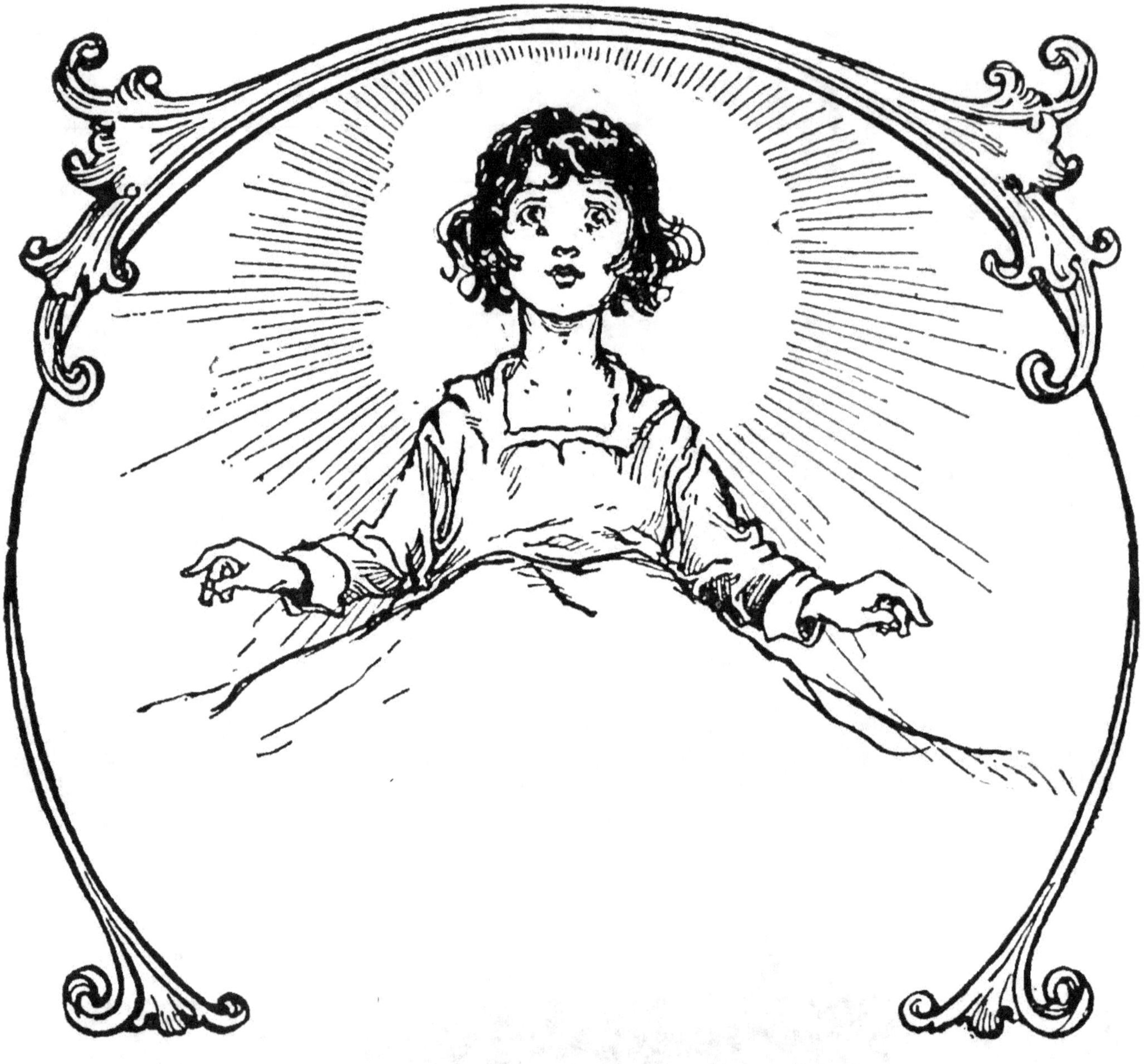

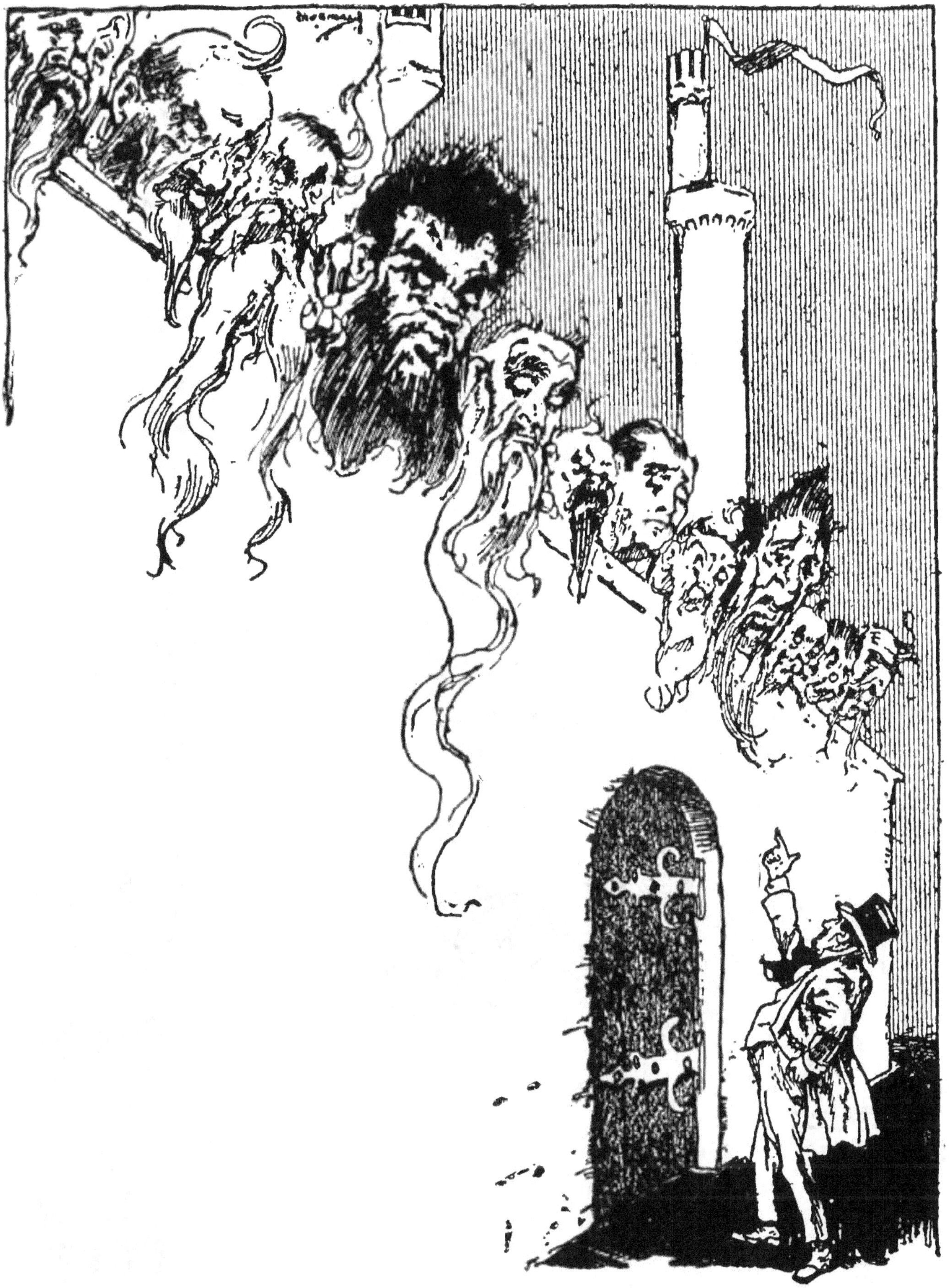

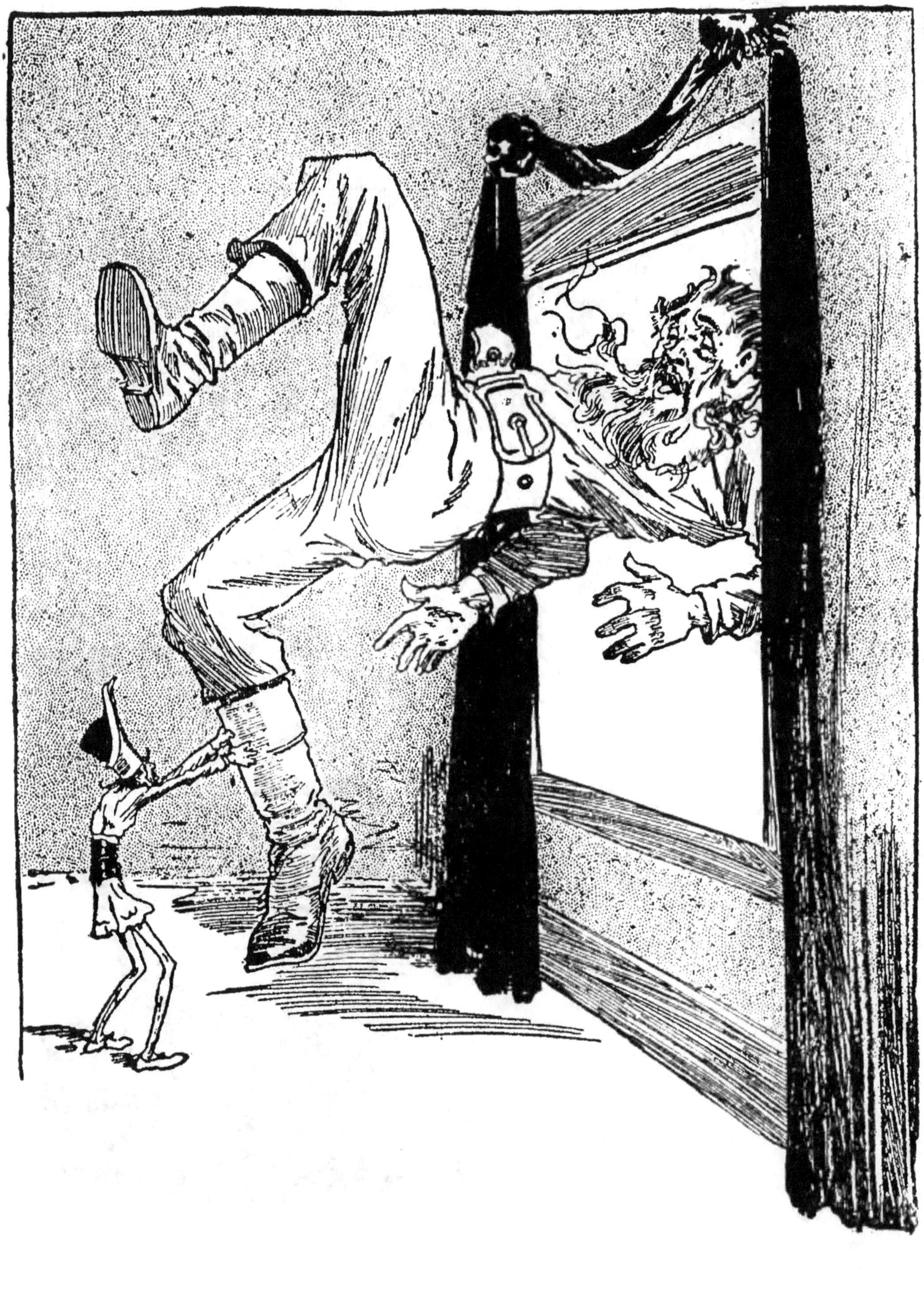

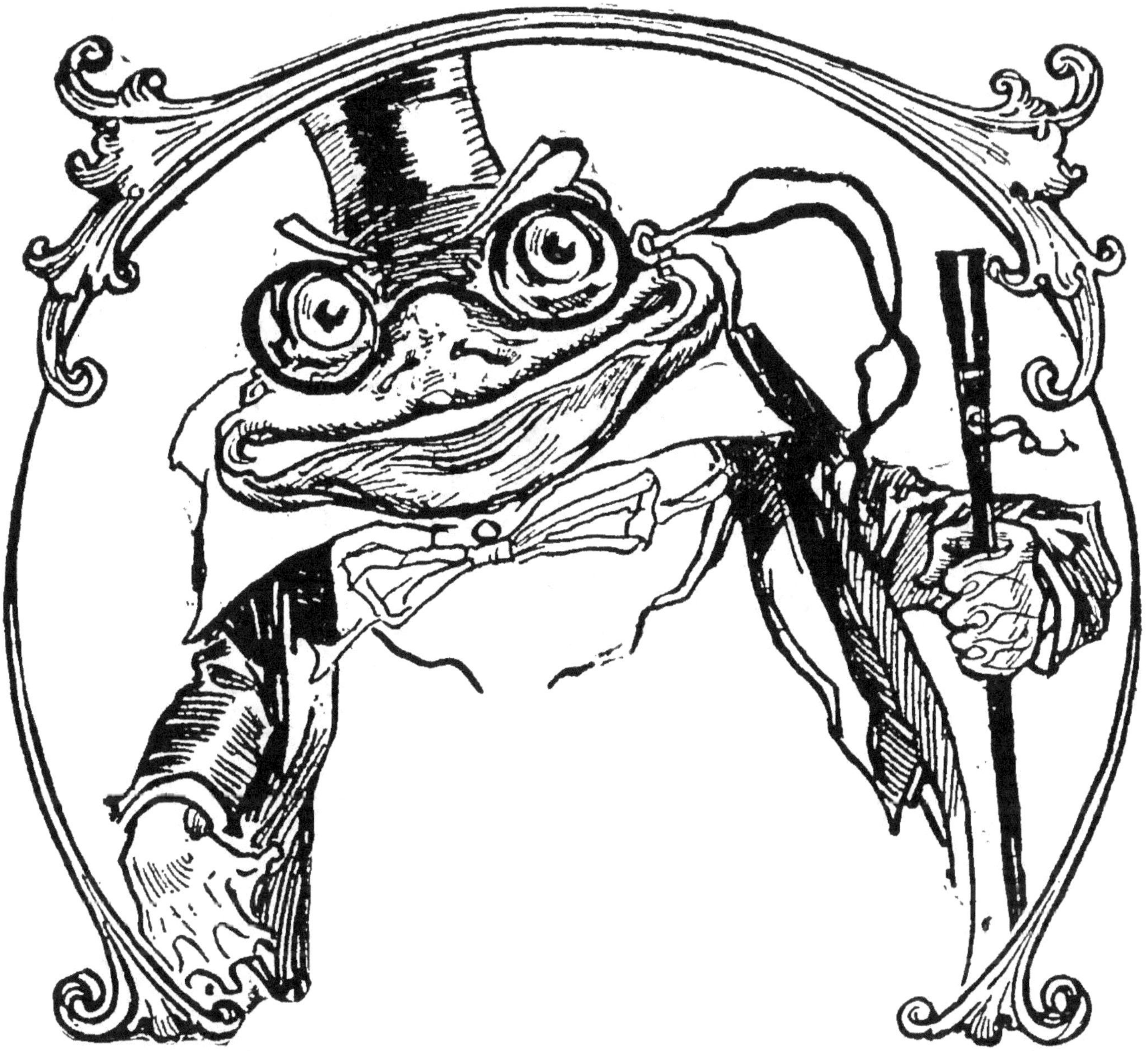

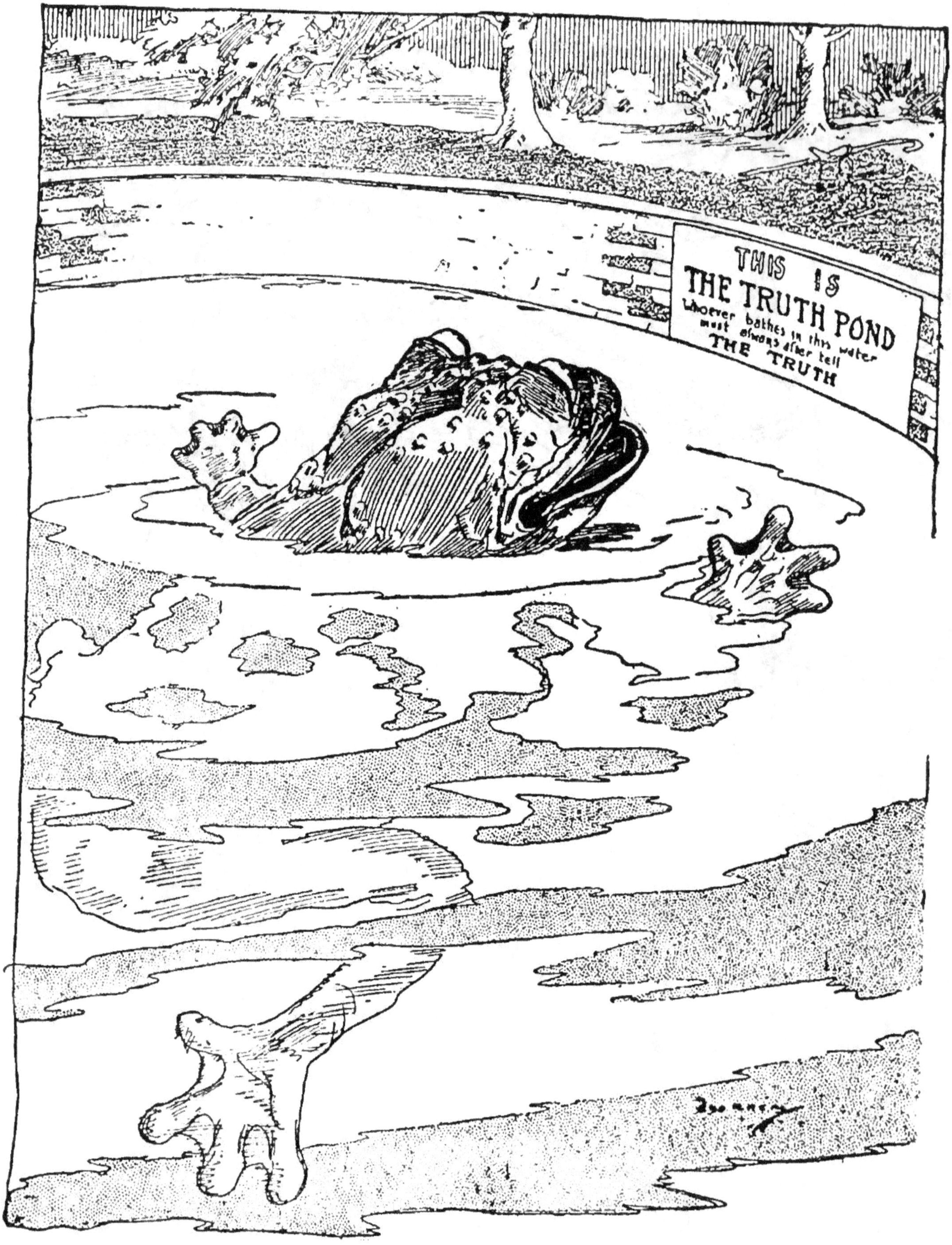
THIS IS
THE TRUTH POND
Whoever bathes in this water
must always after tell
THE TRUTH

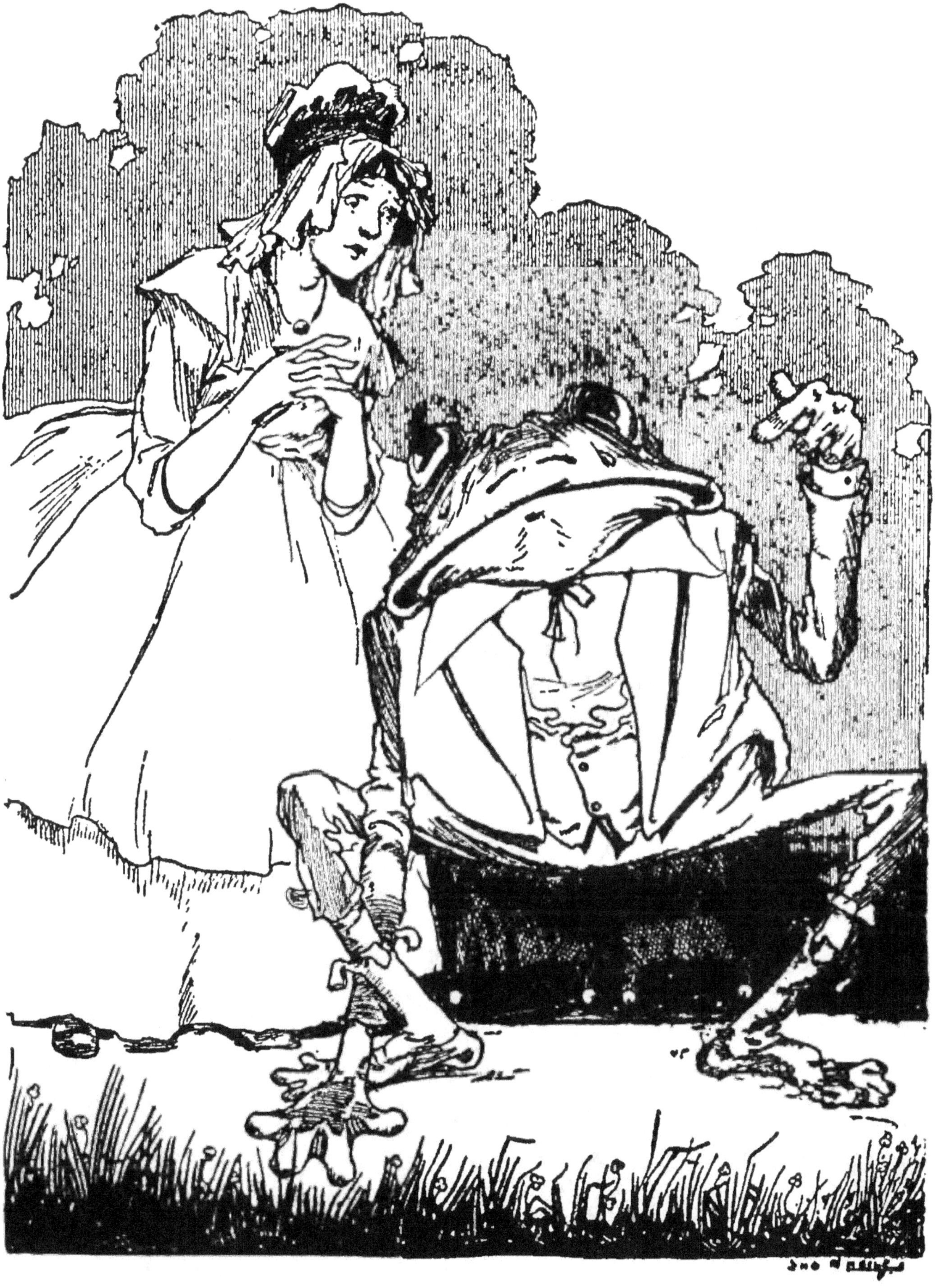

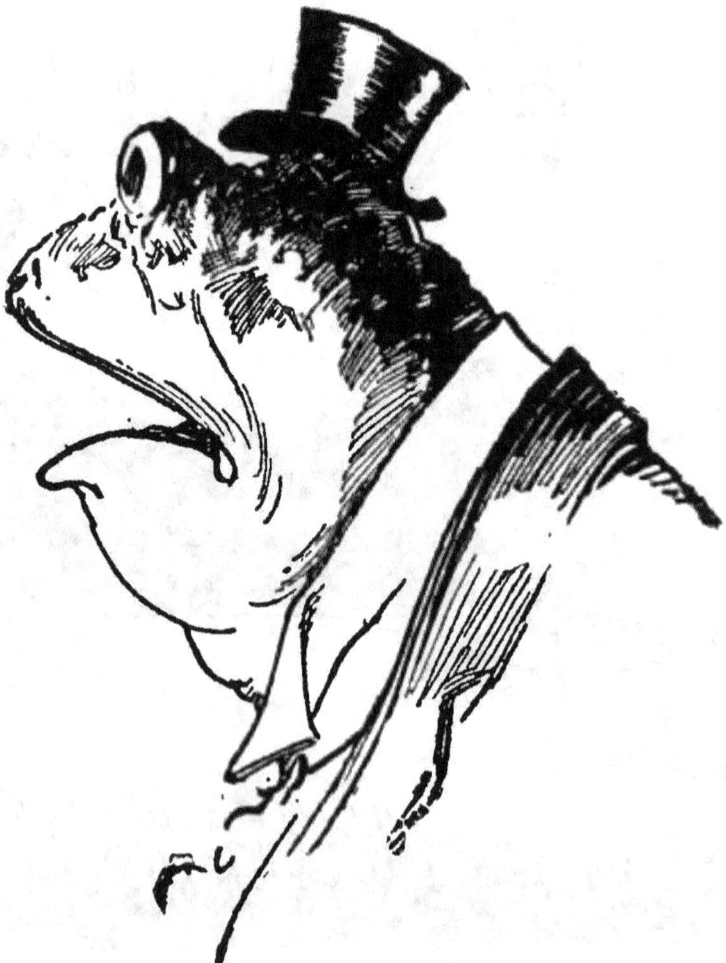

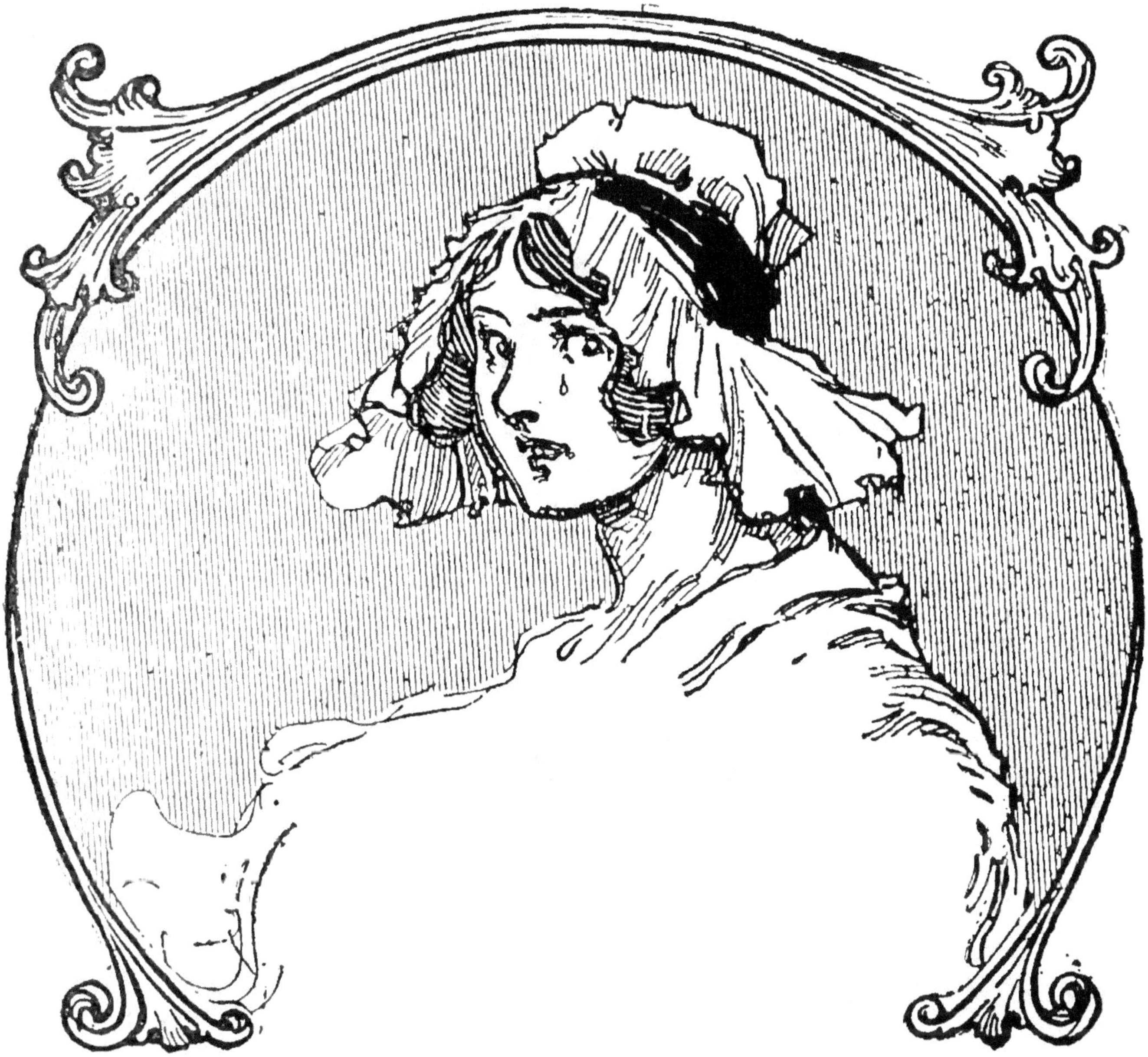

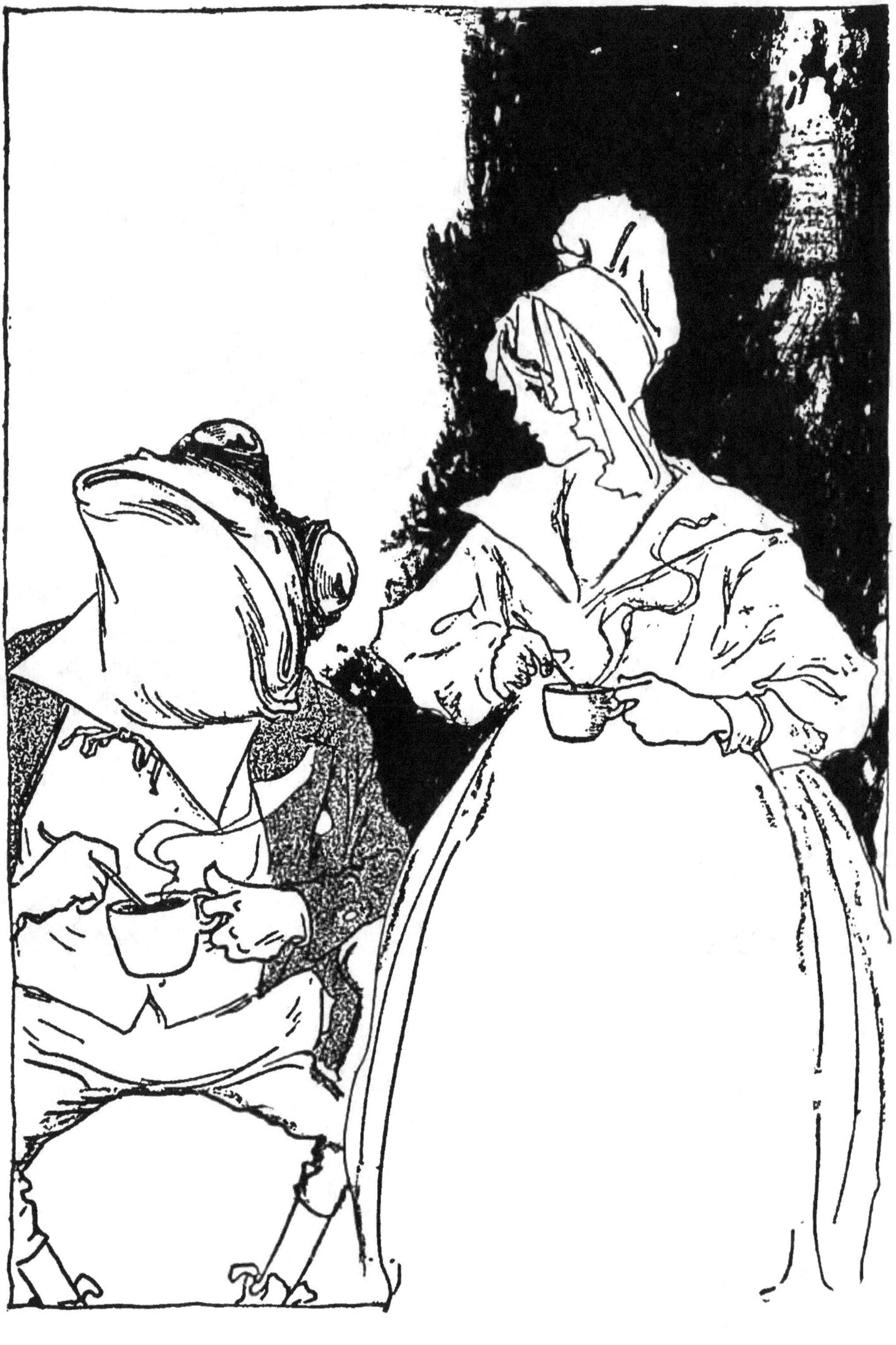

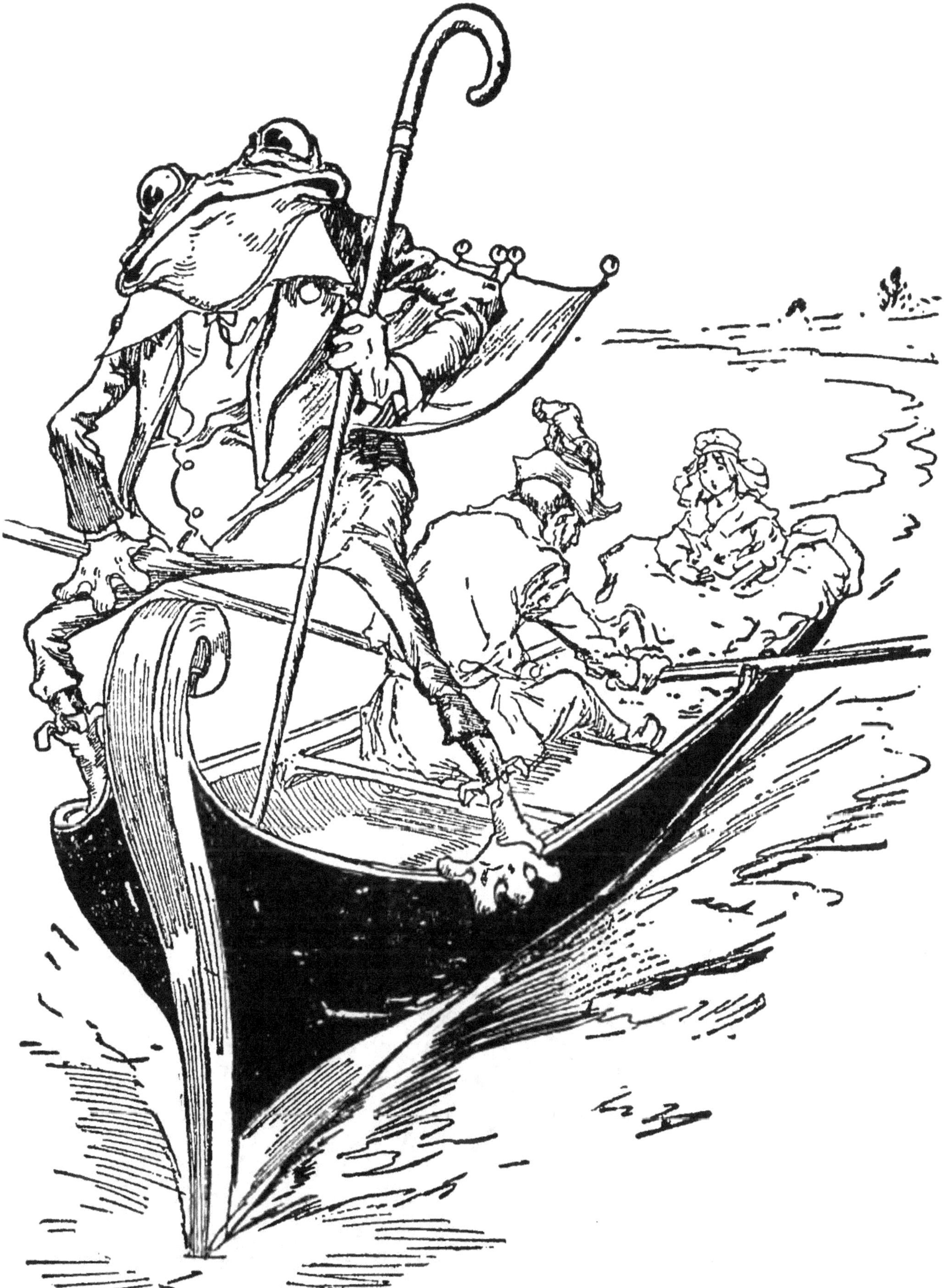

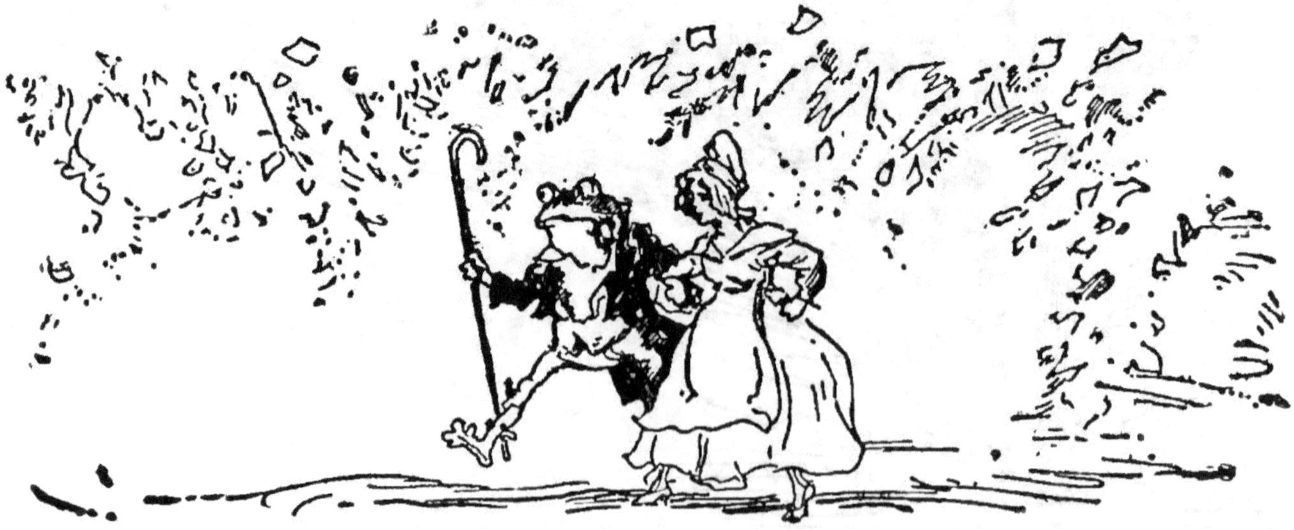

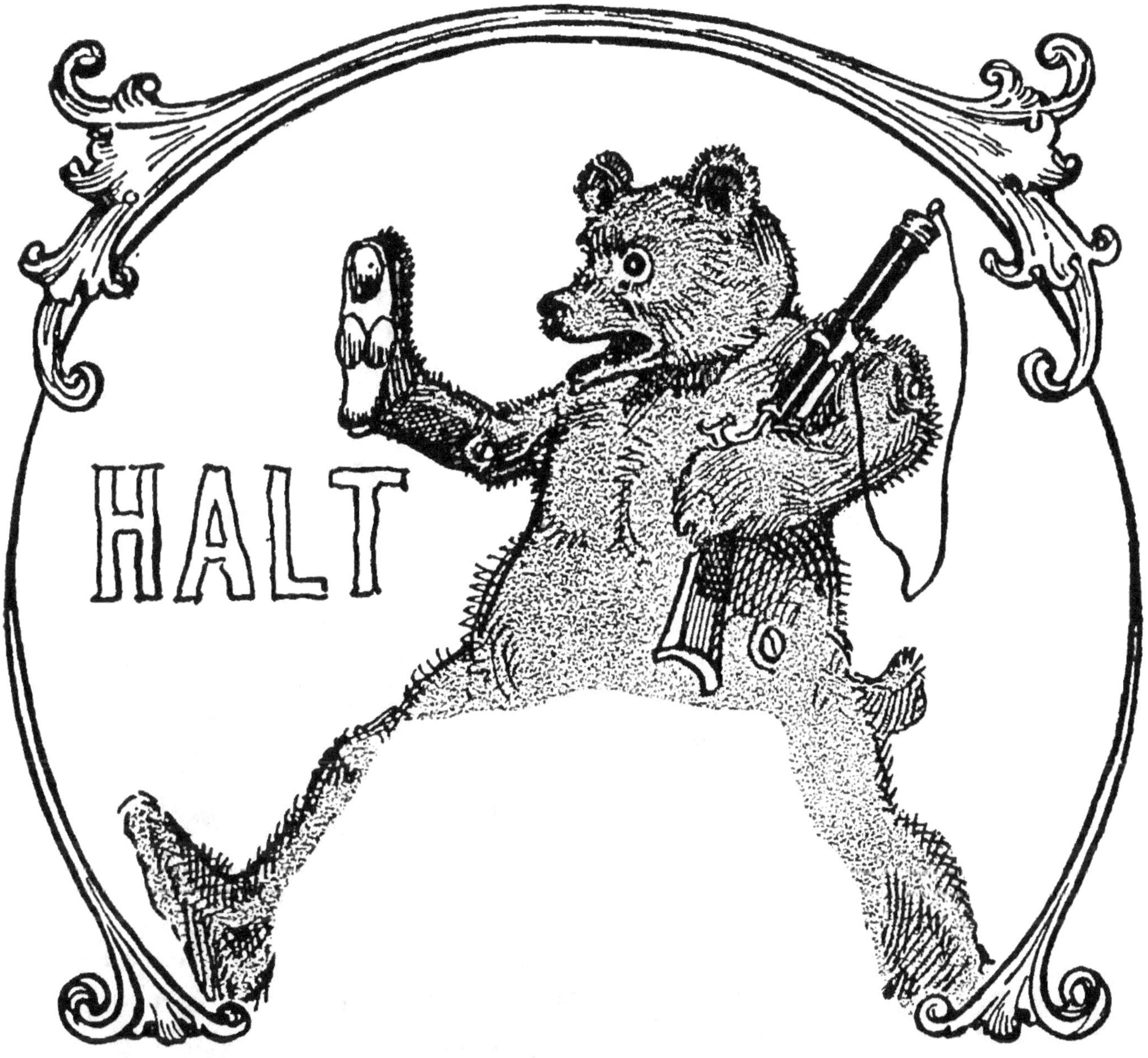
HALT

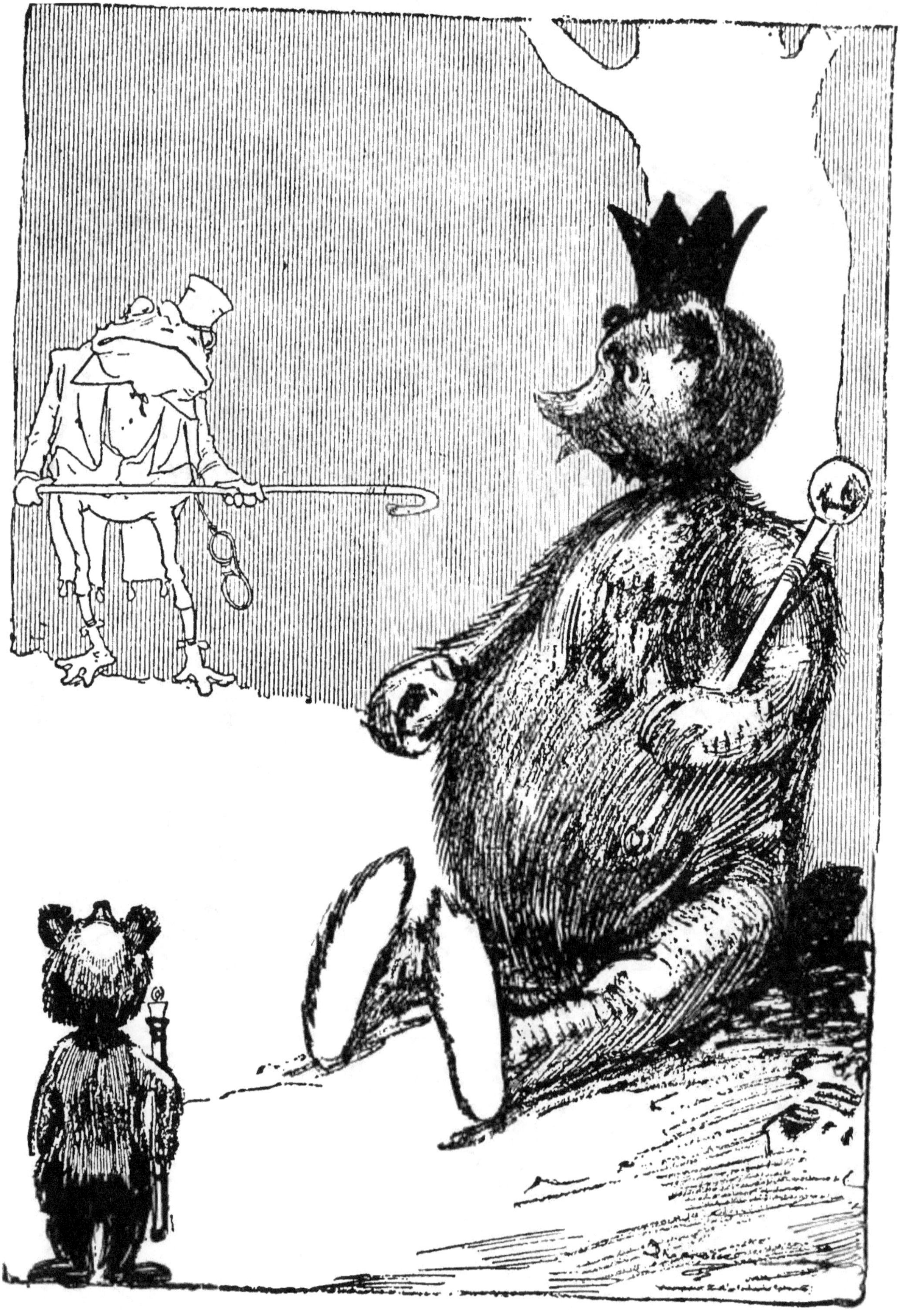

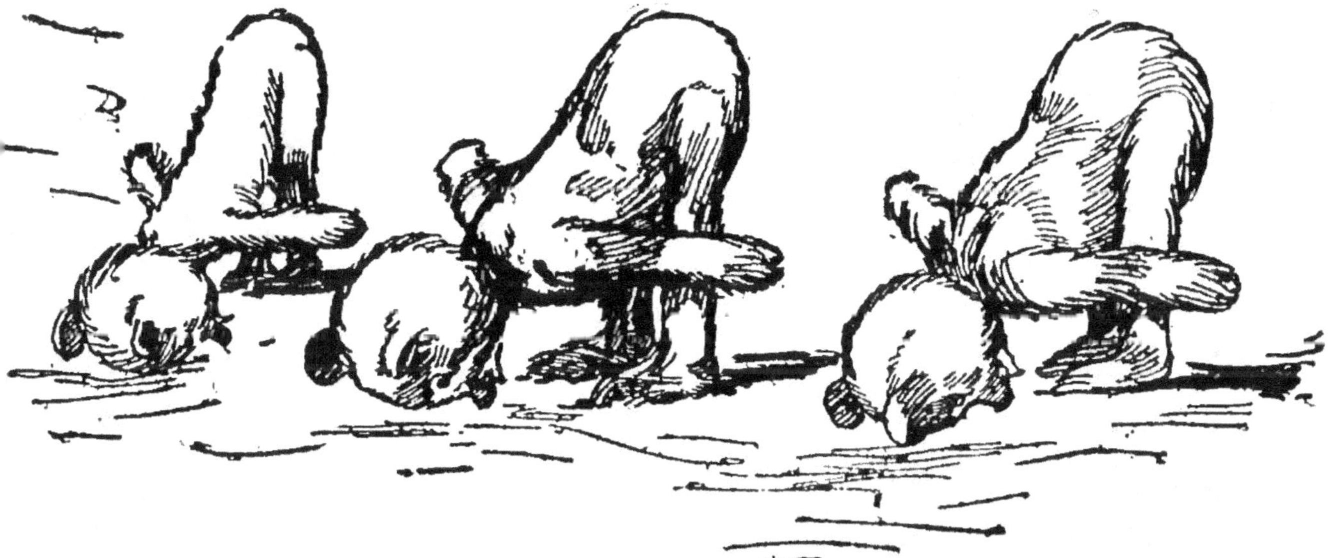

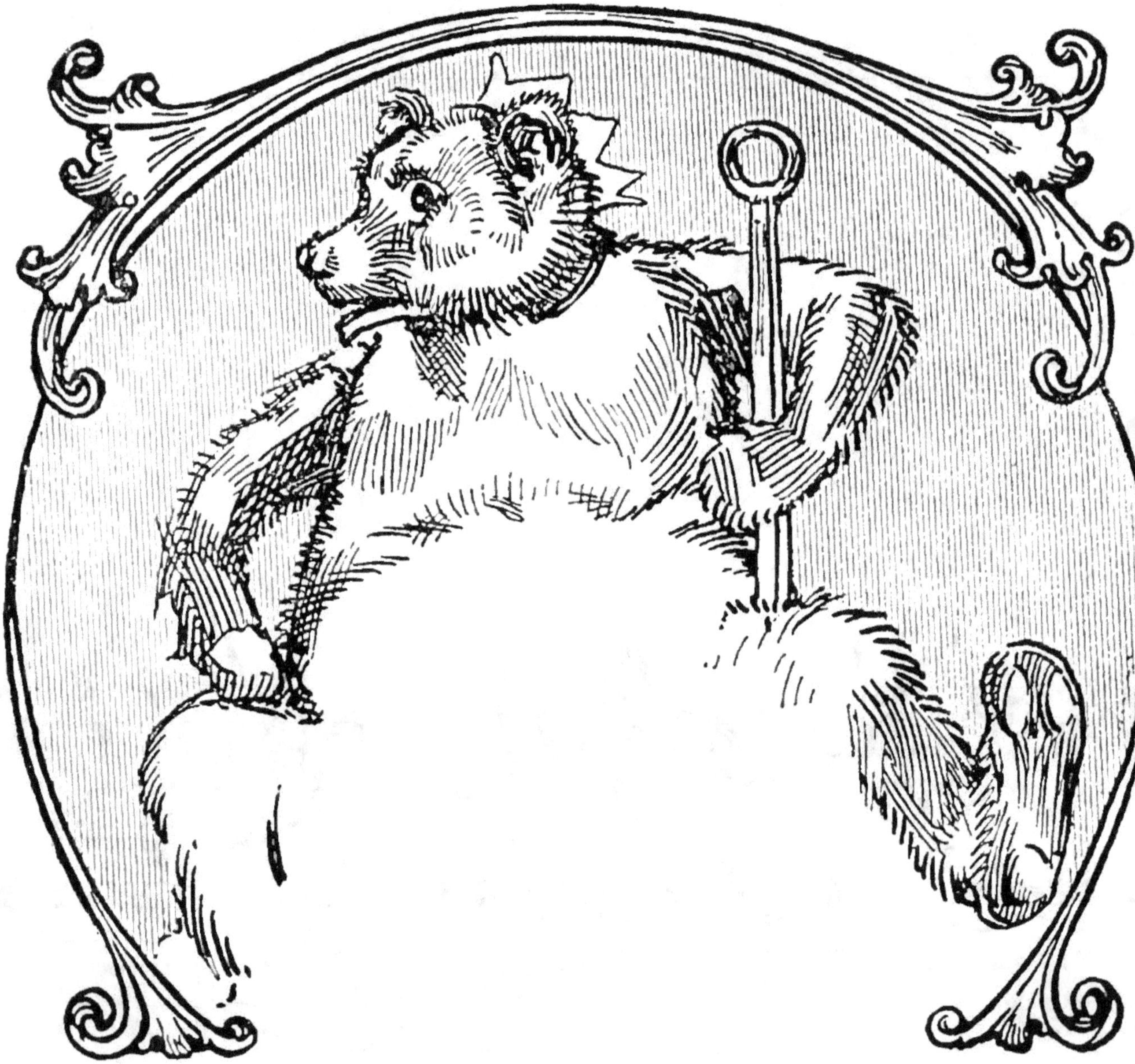

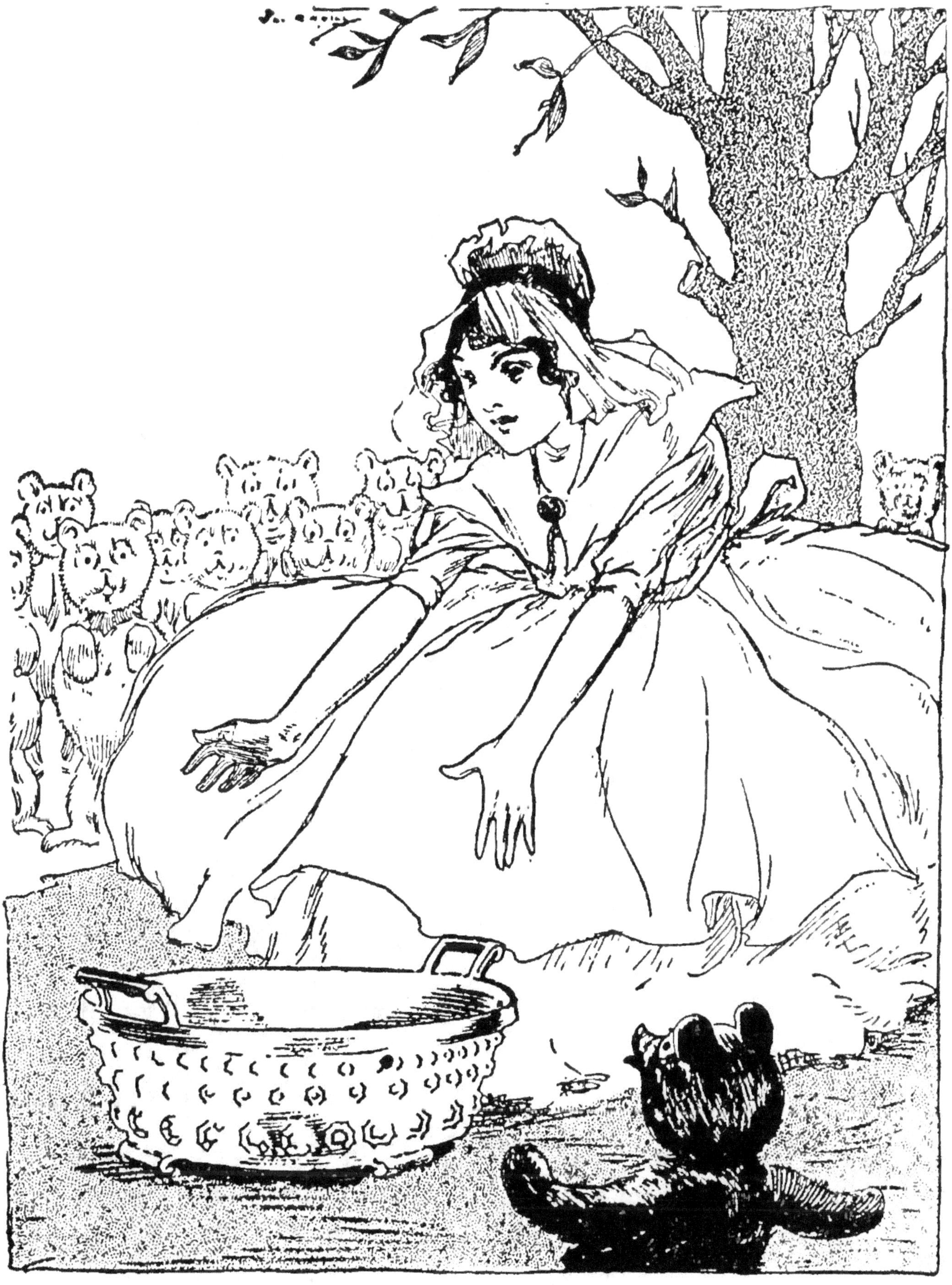

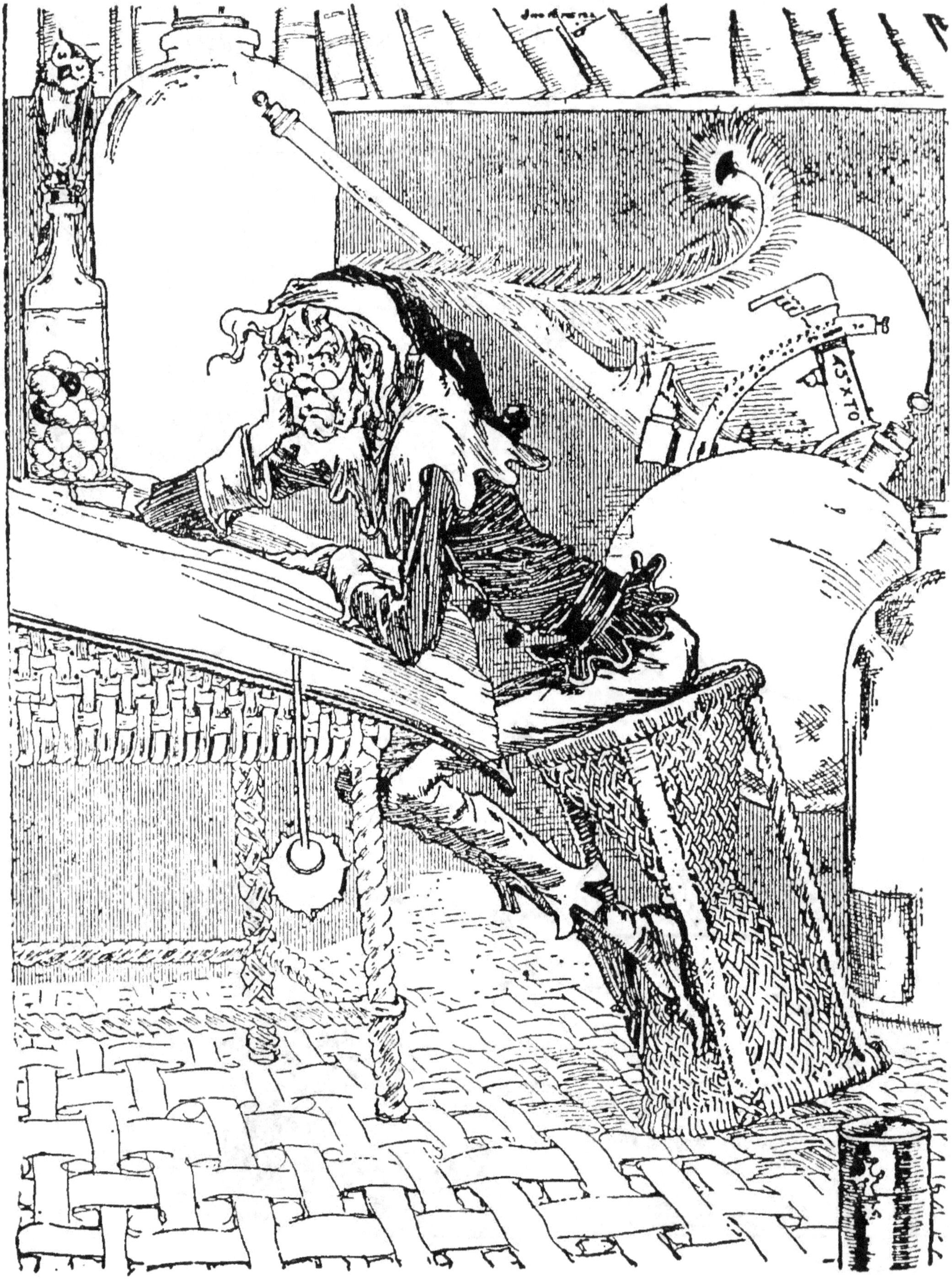

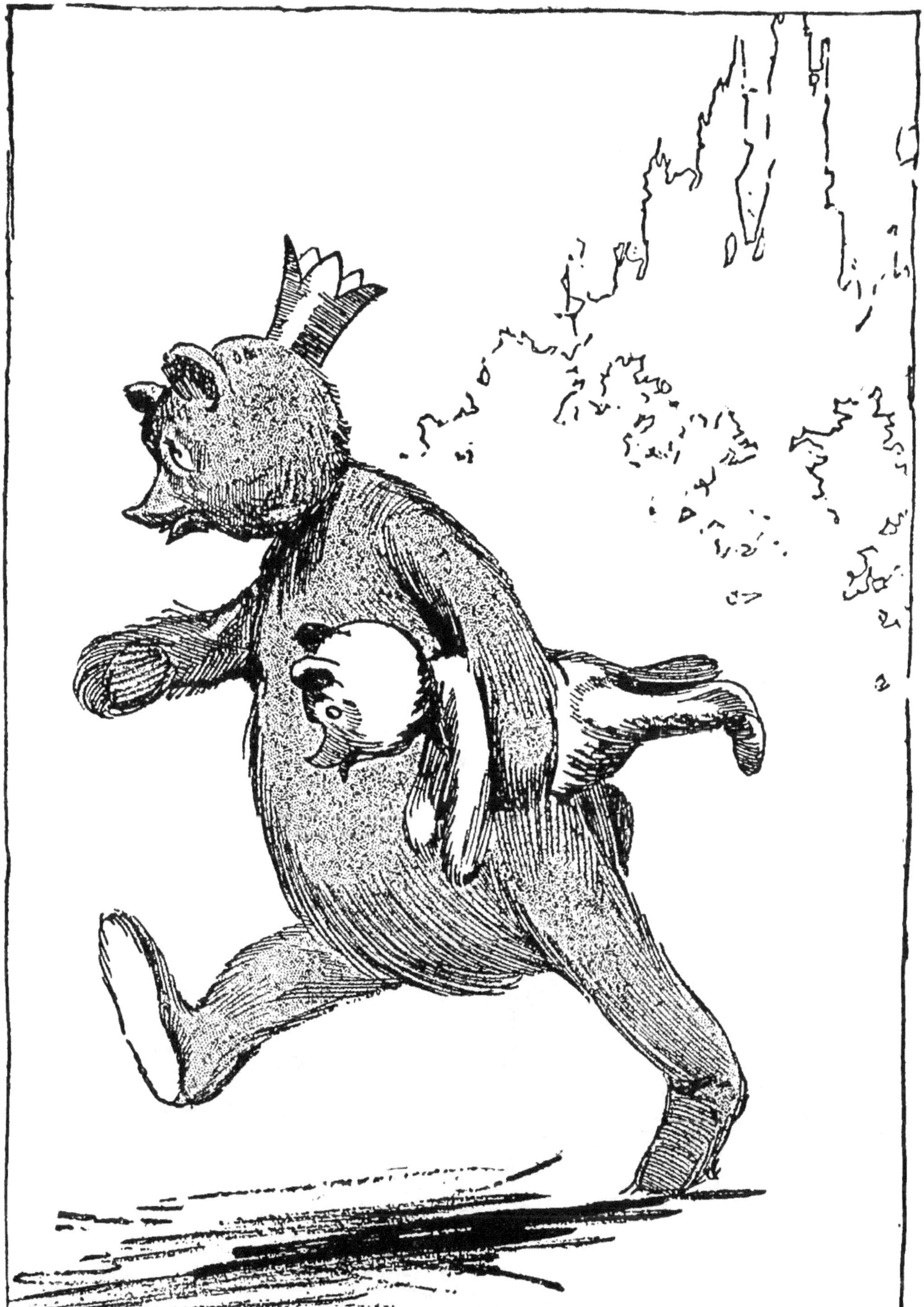

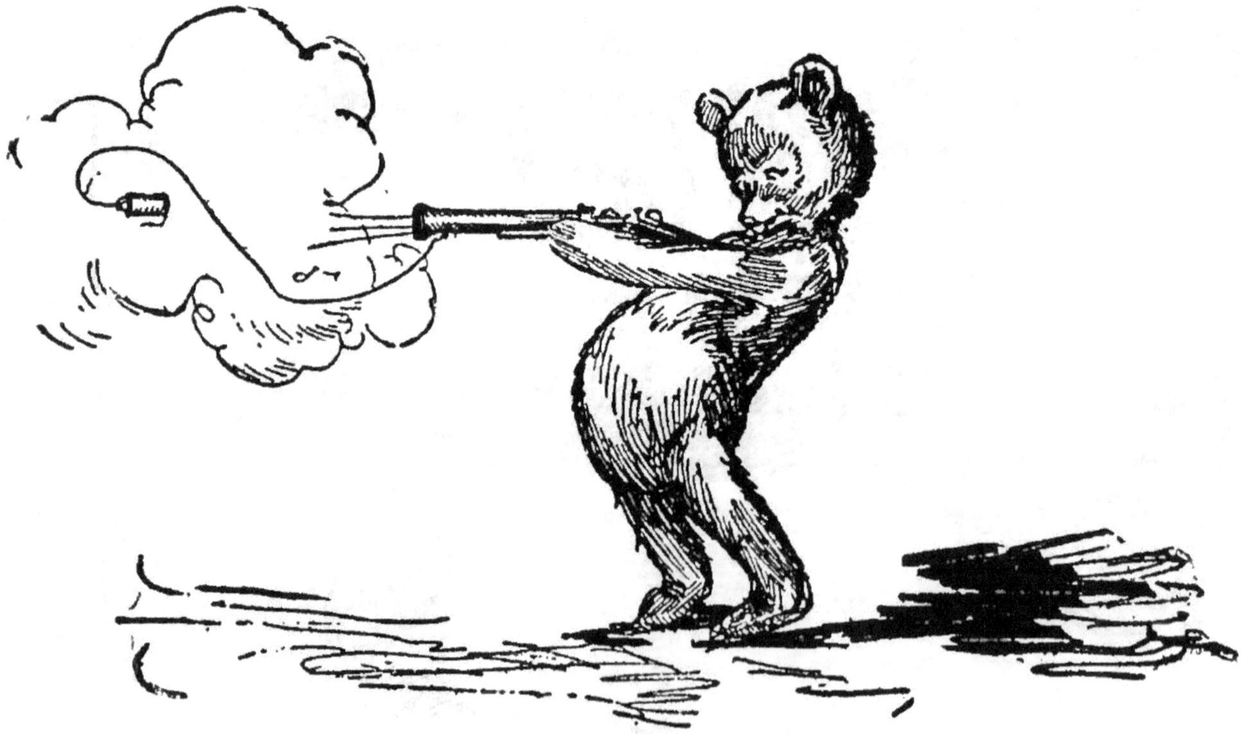

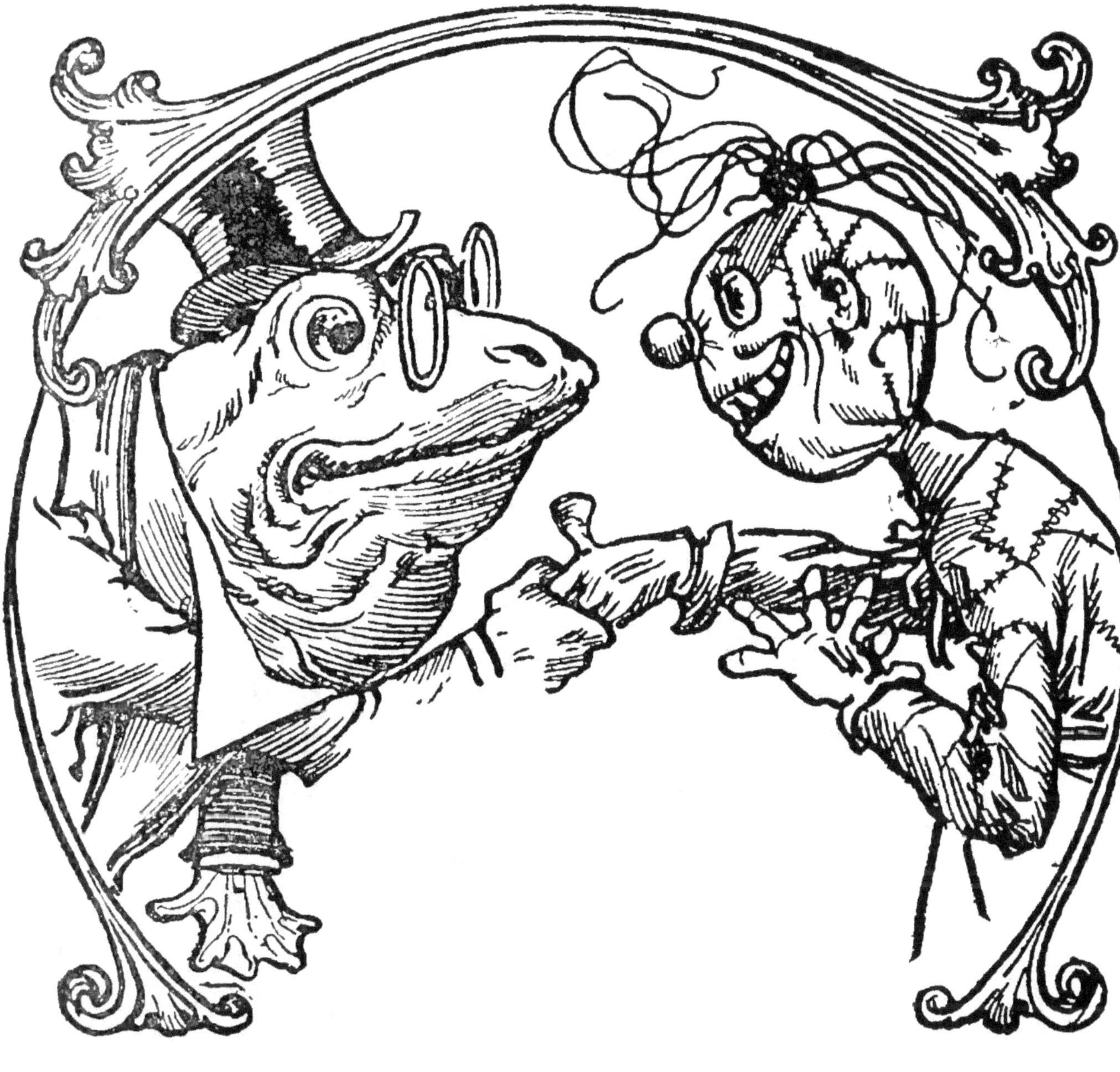

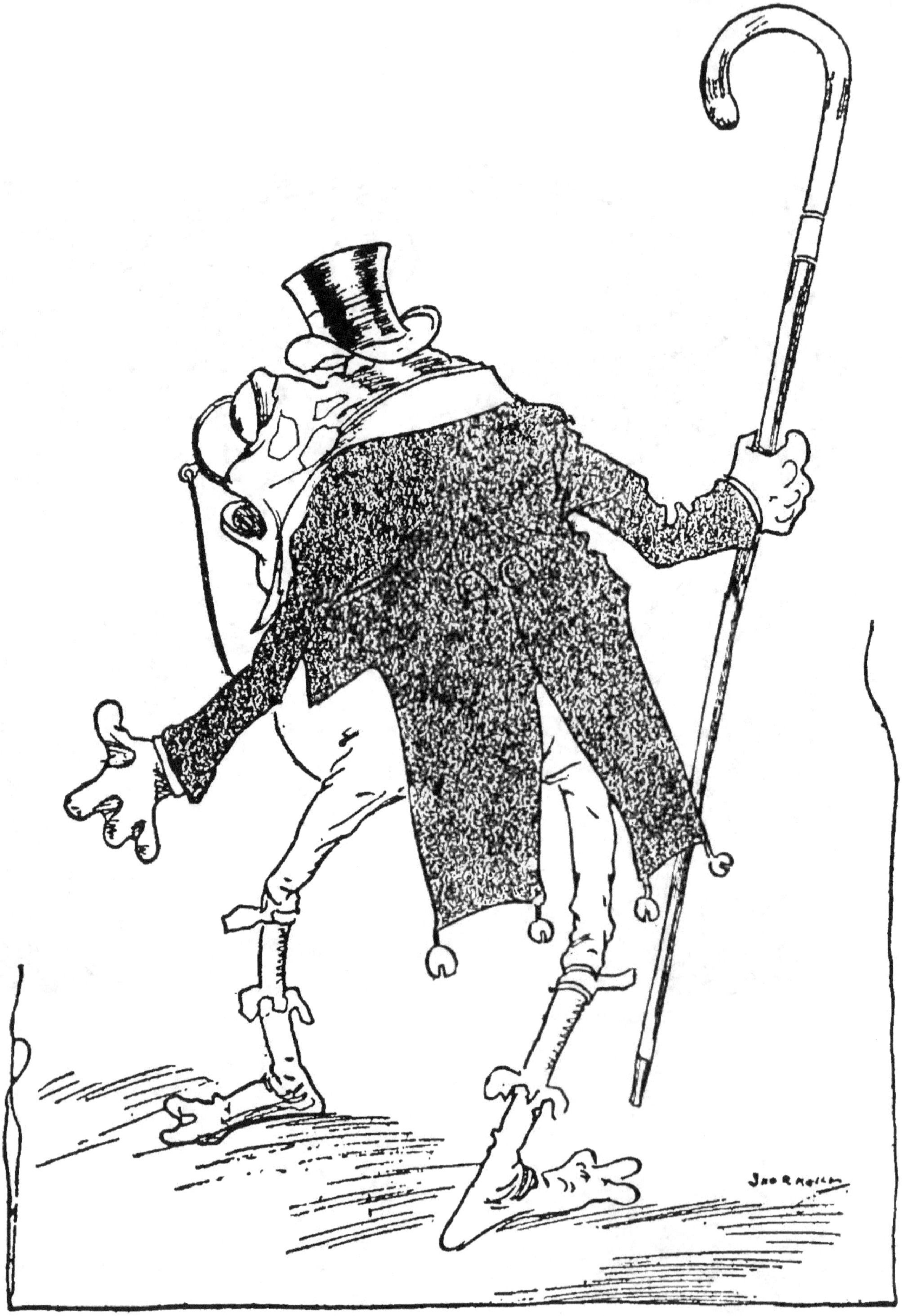

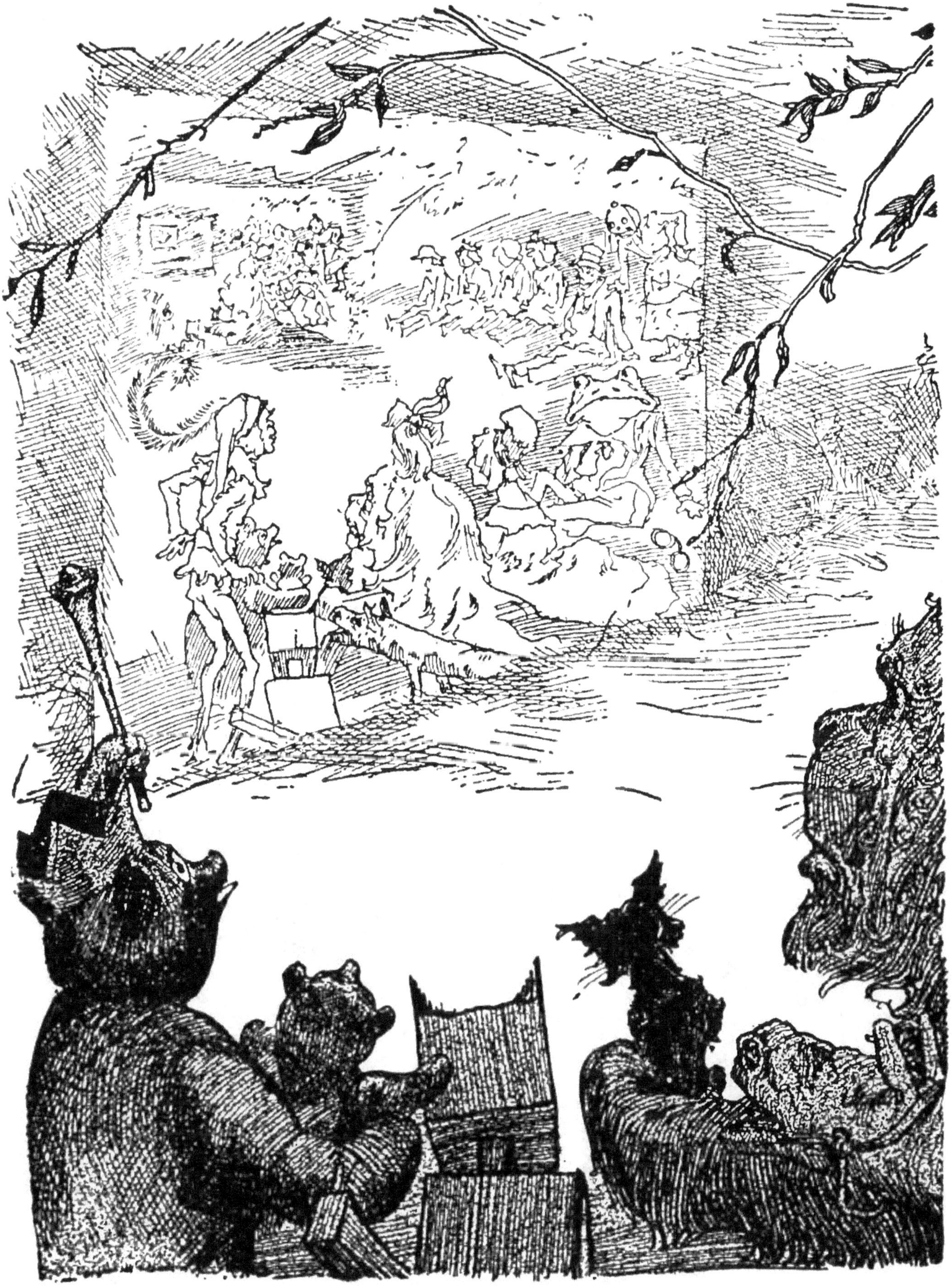

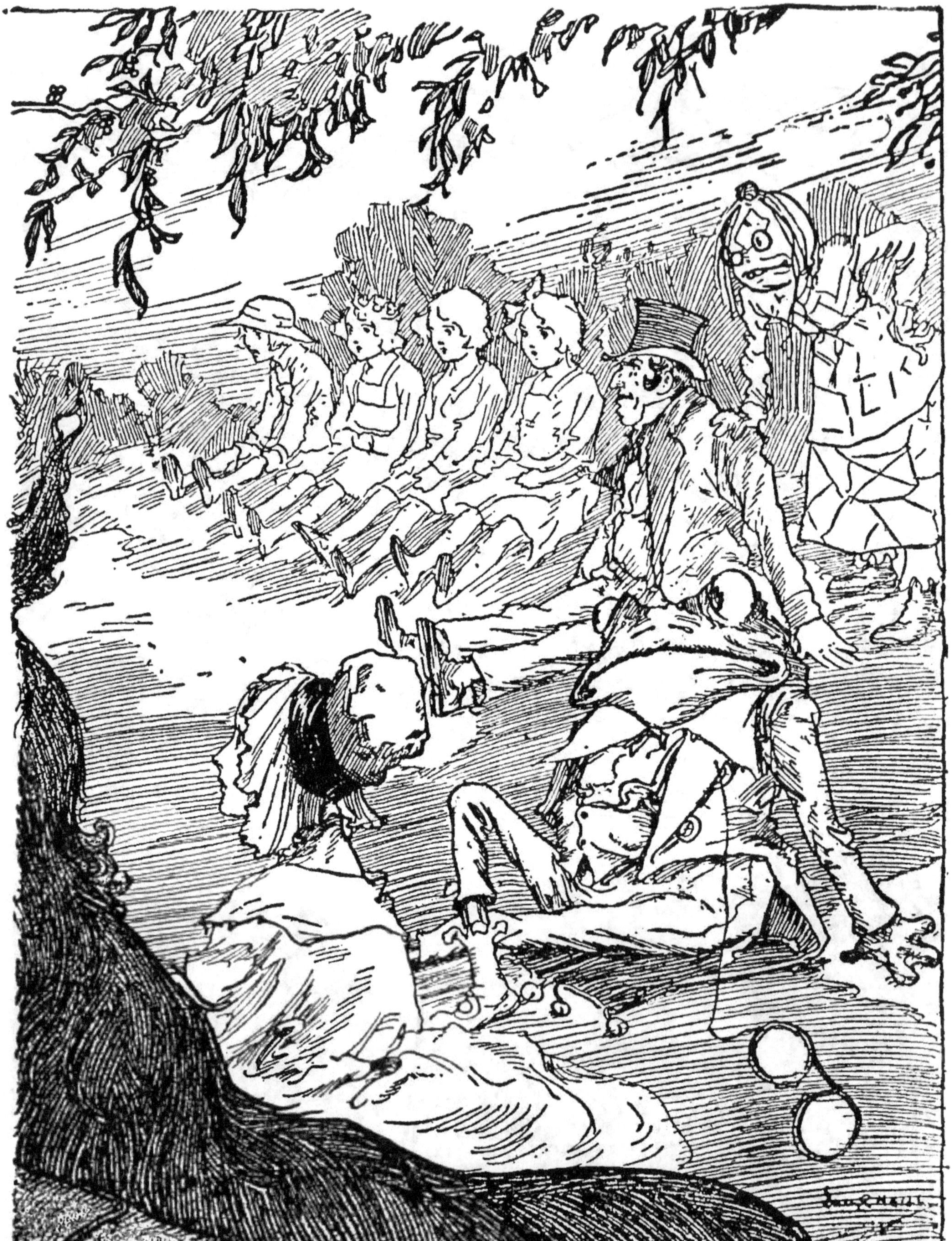

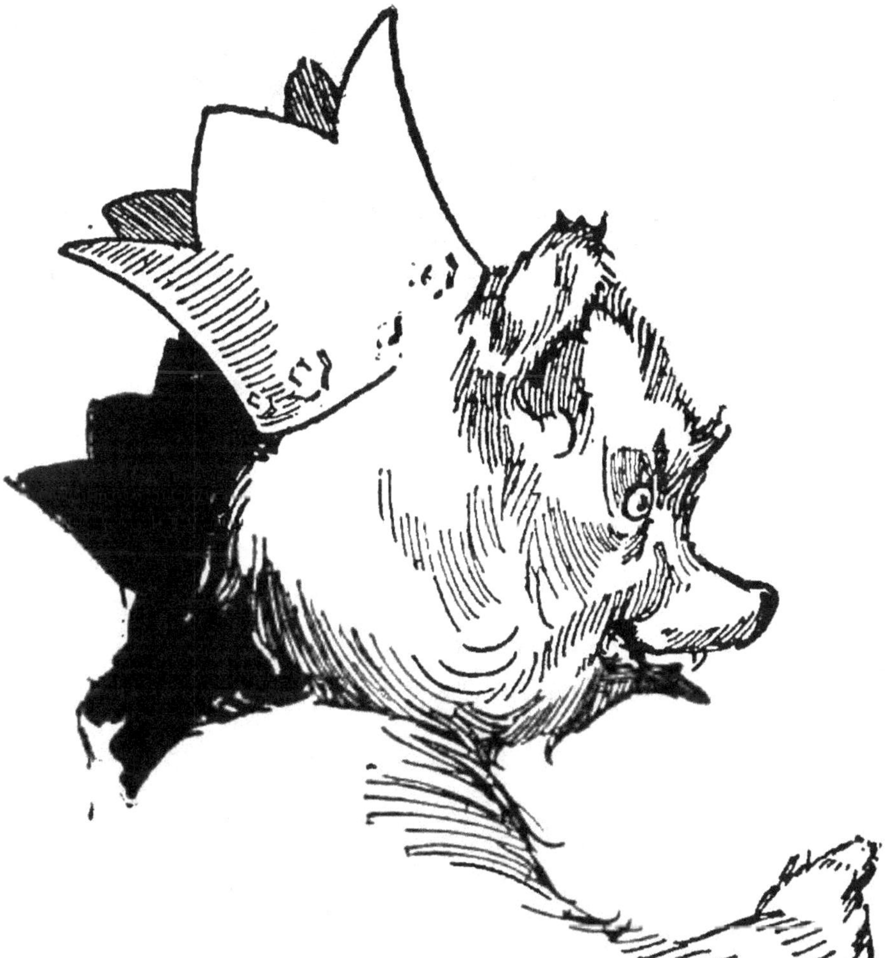

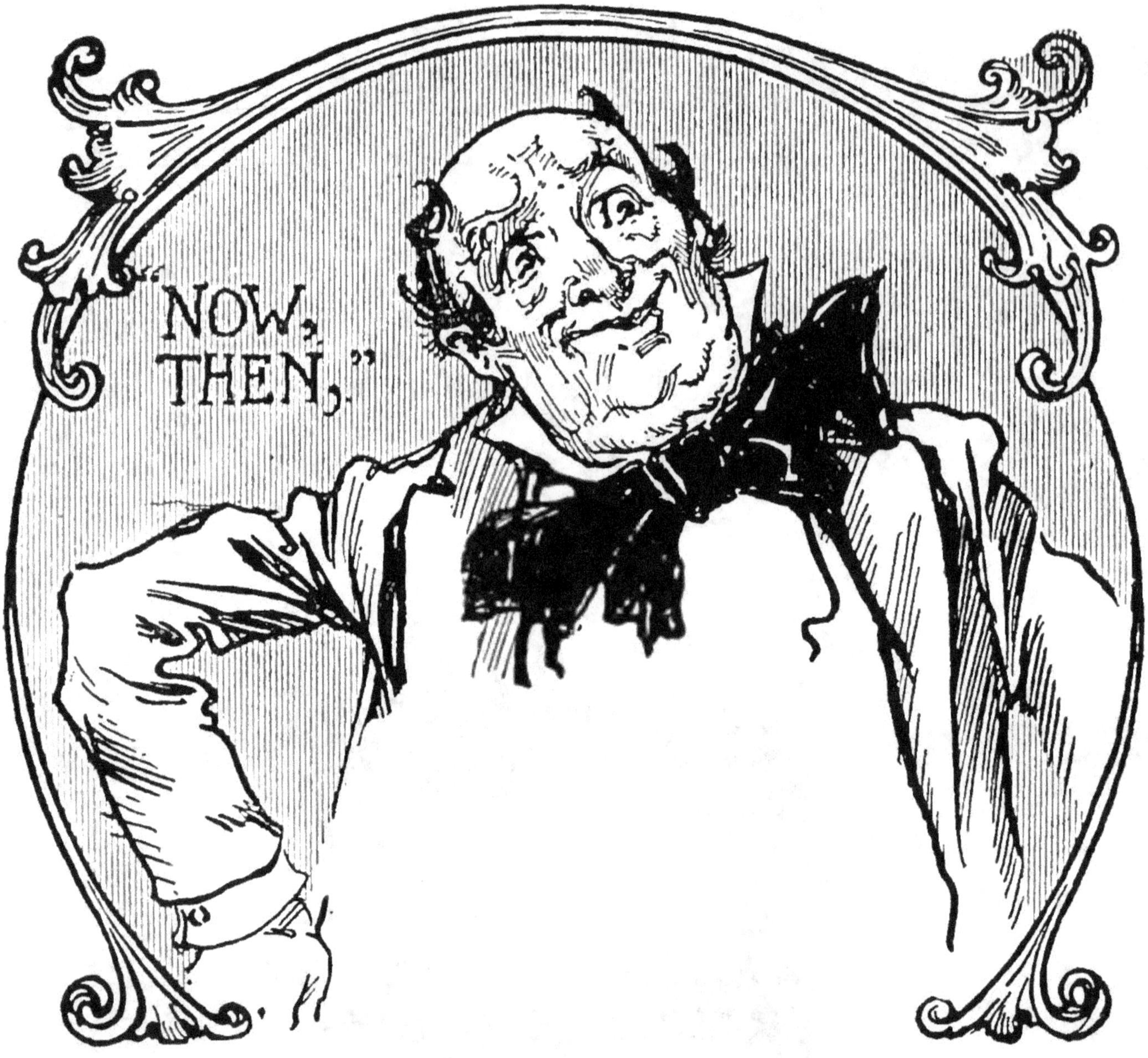
"NOW, THEN,"

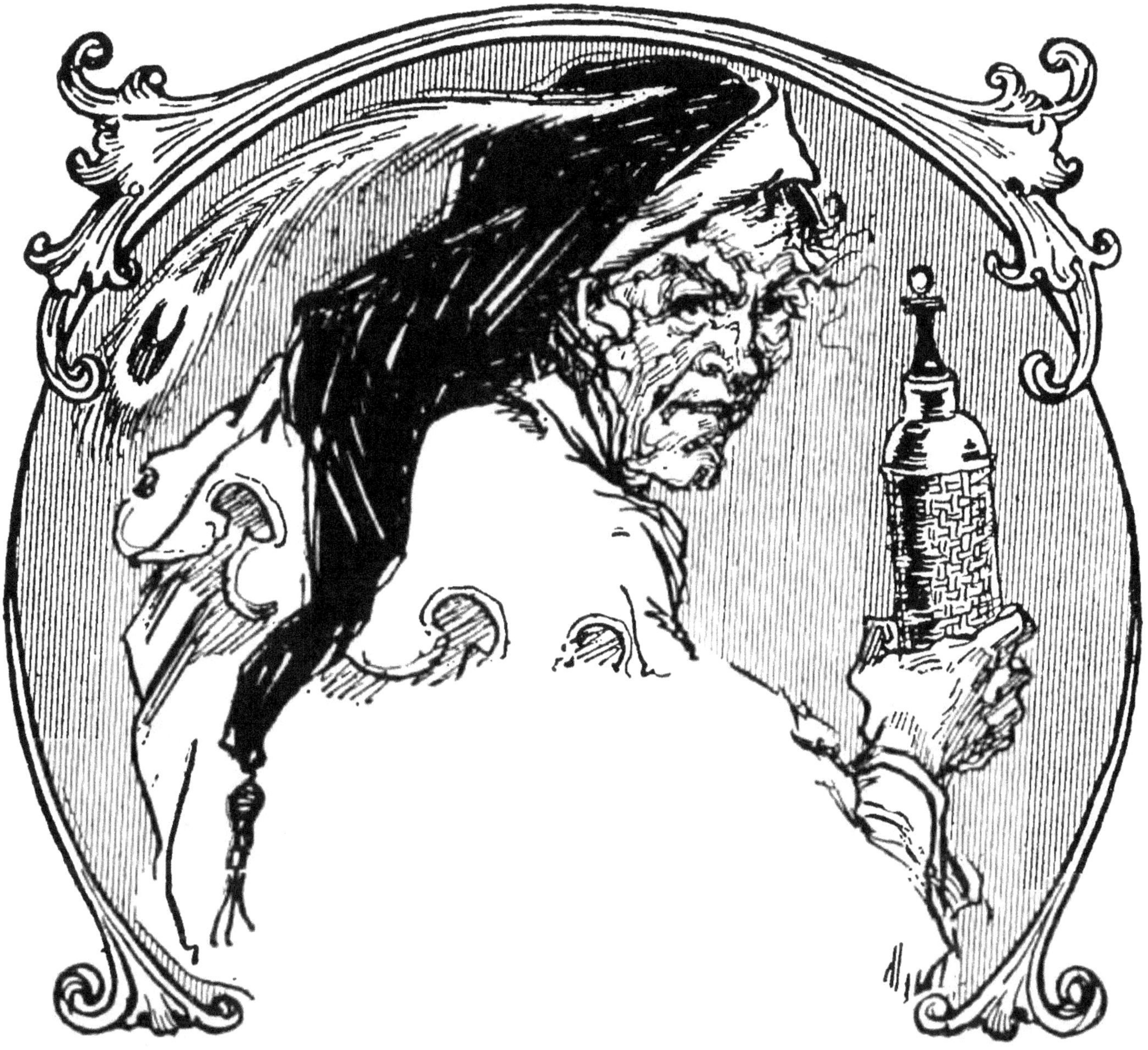

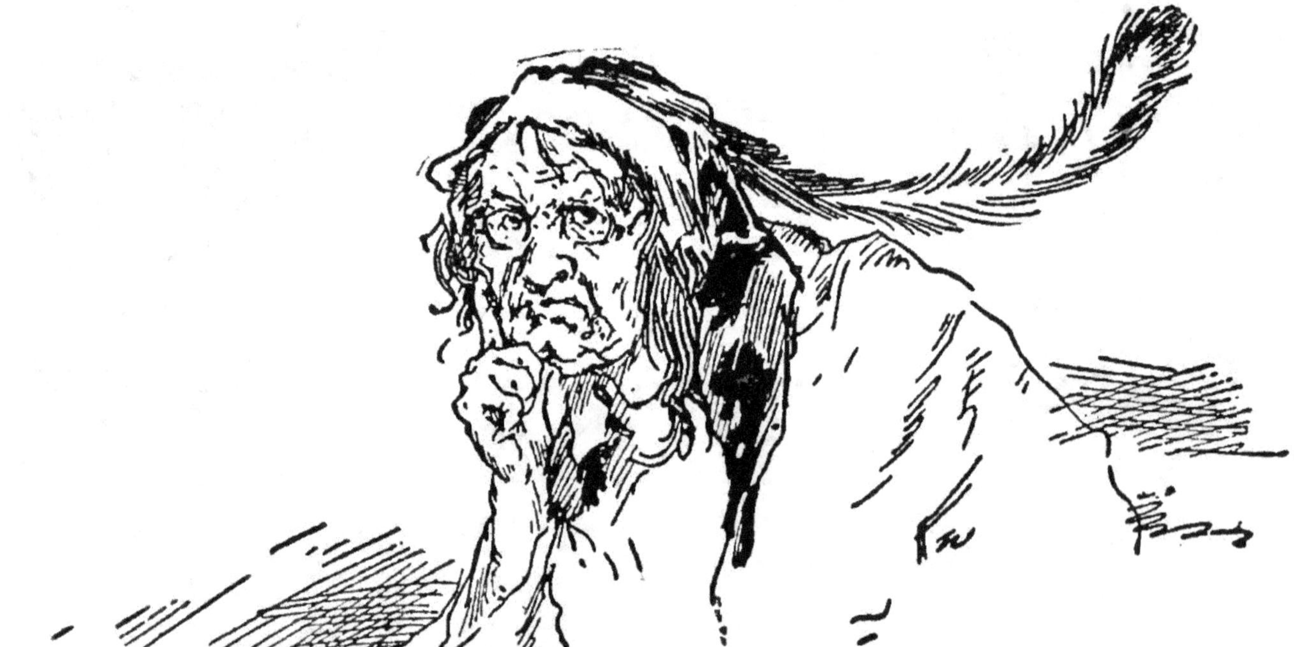

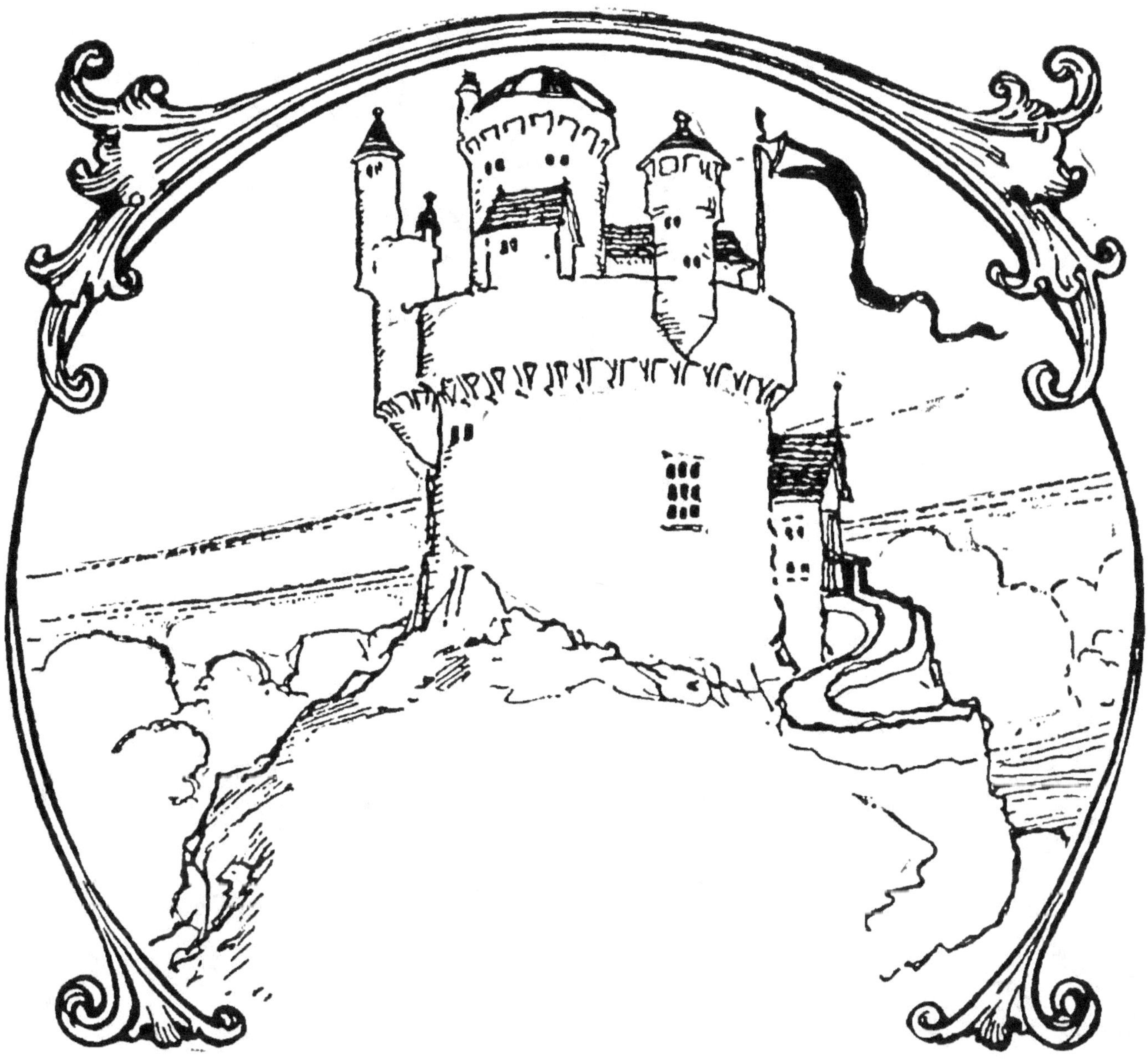

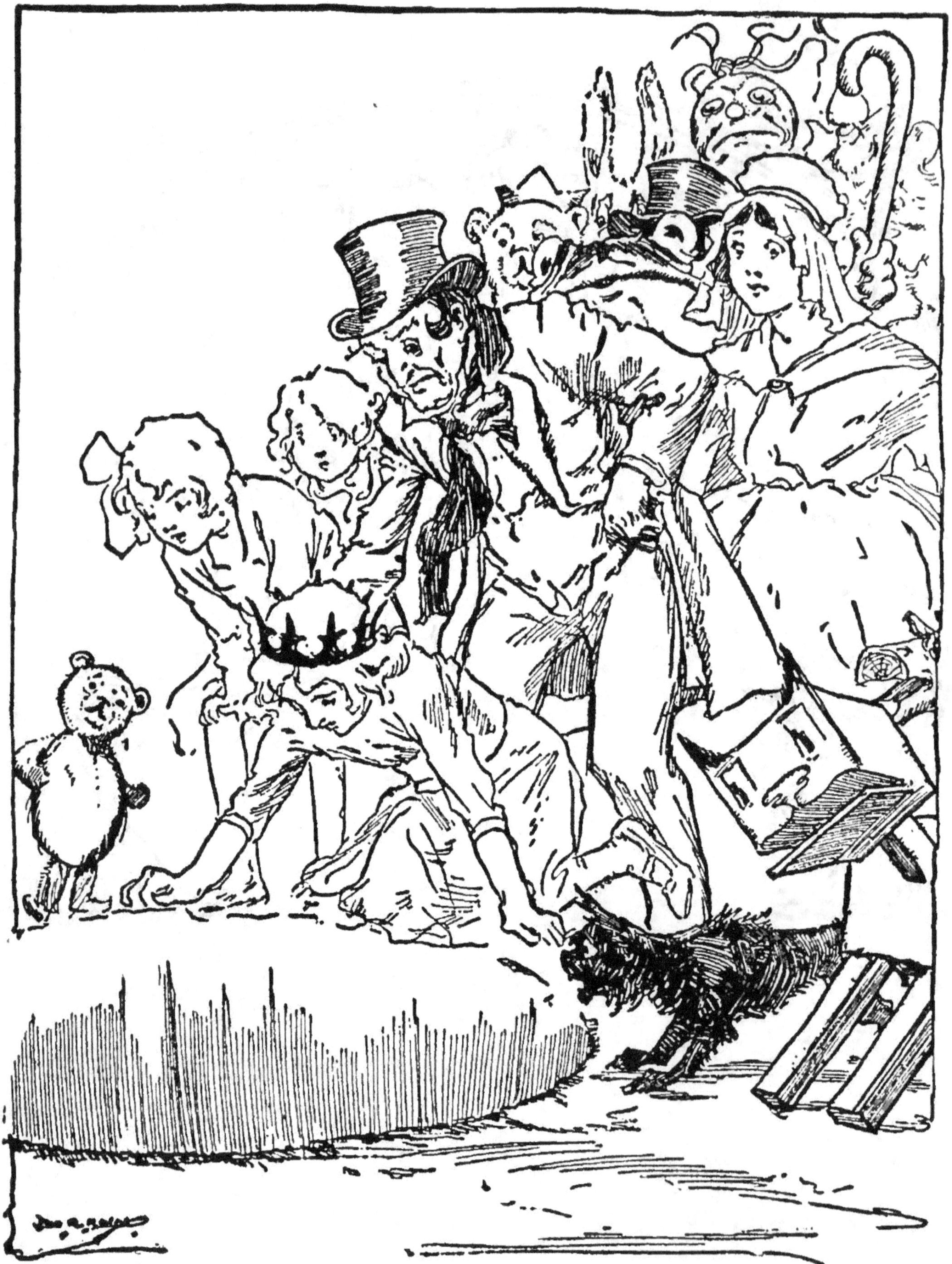

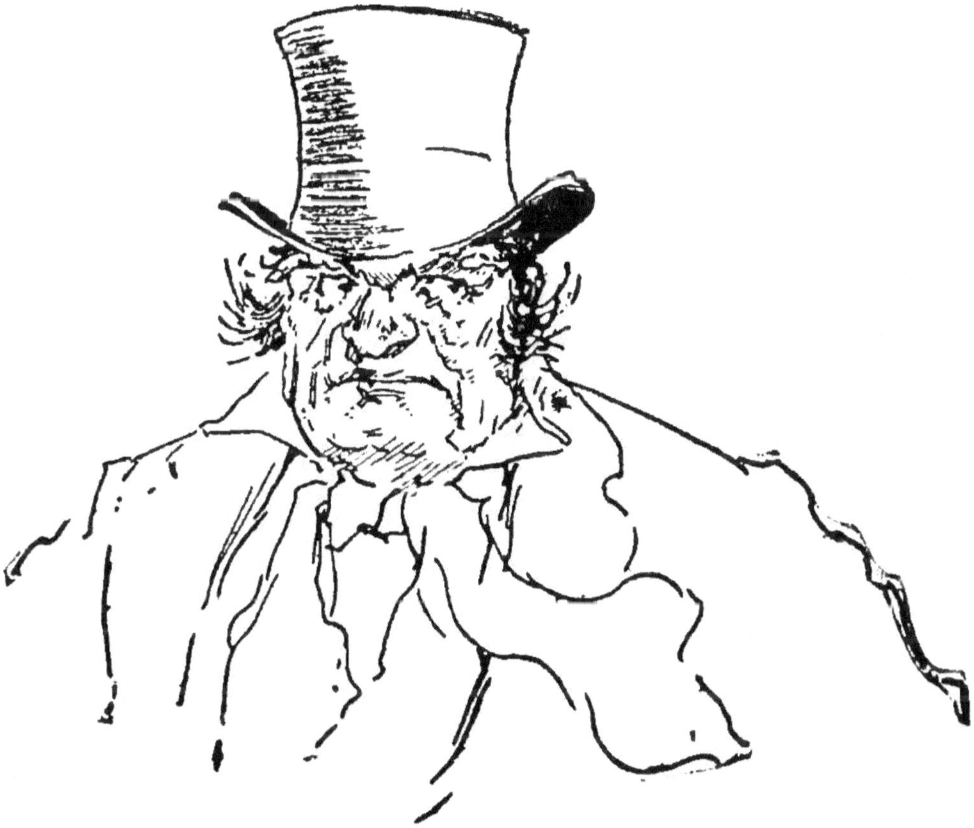

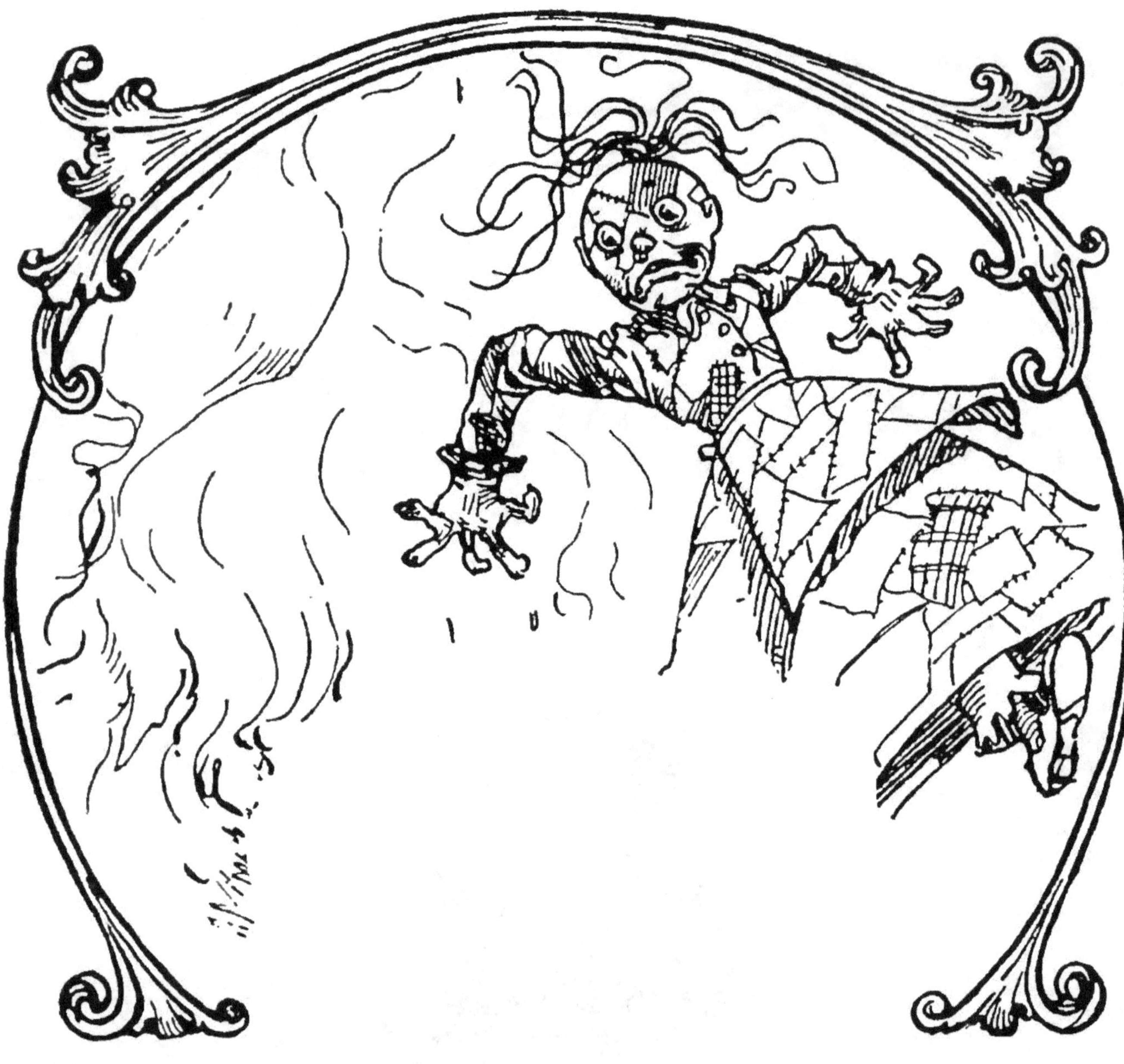

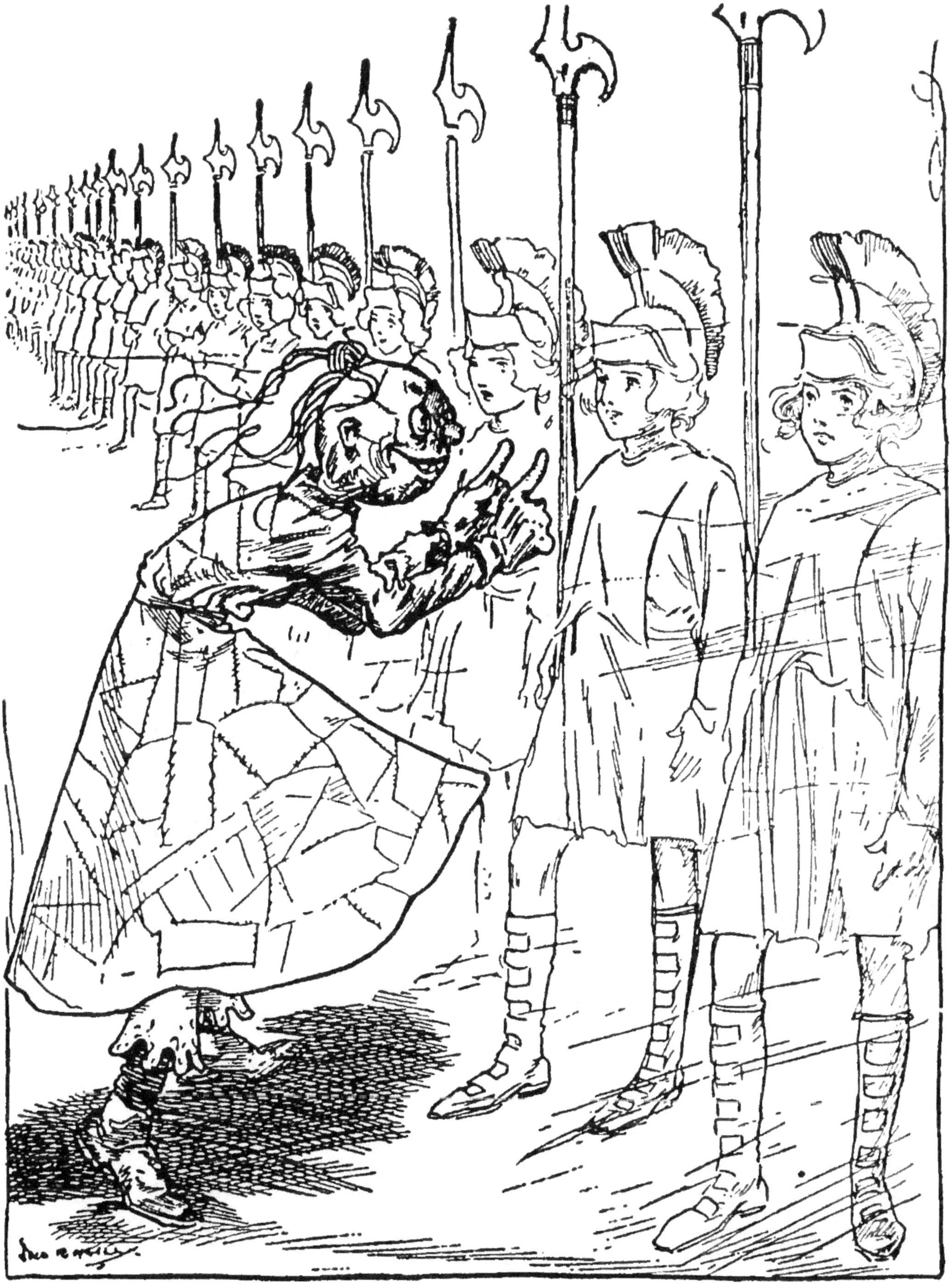

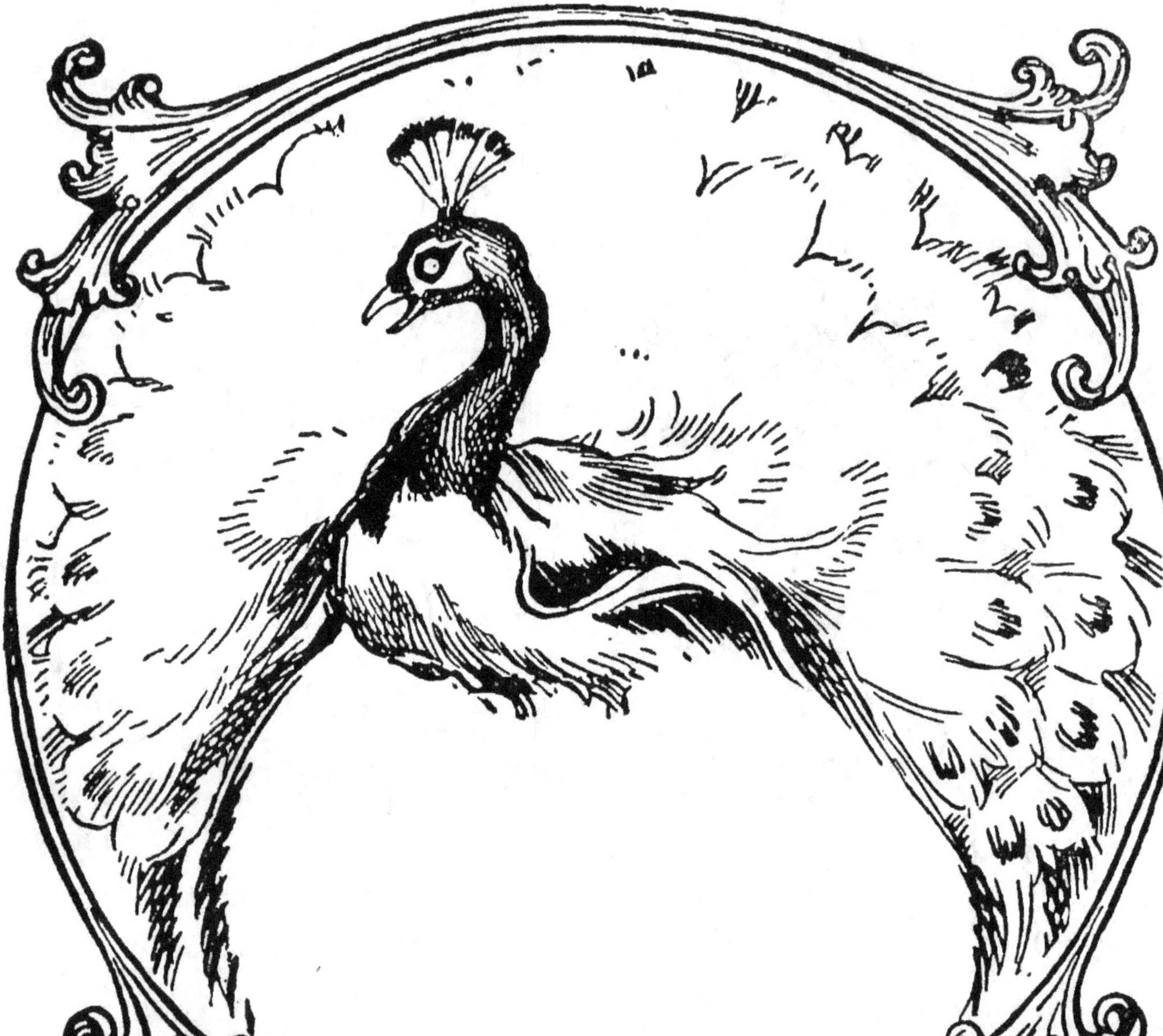

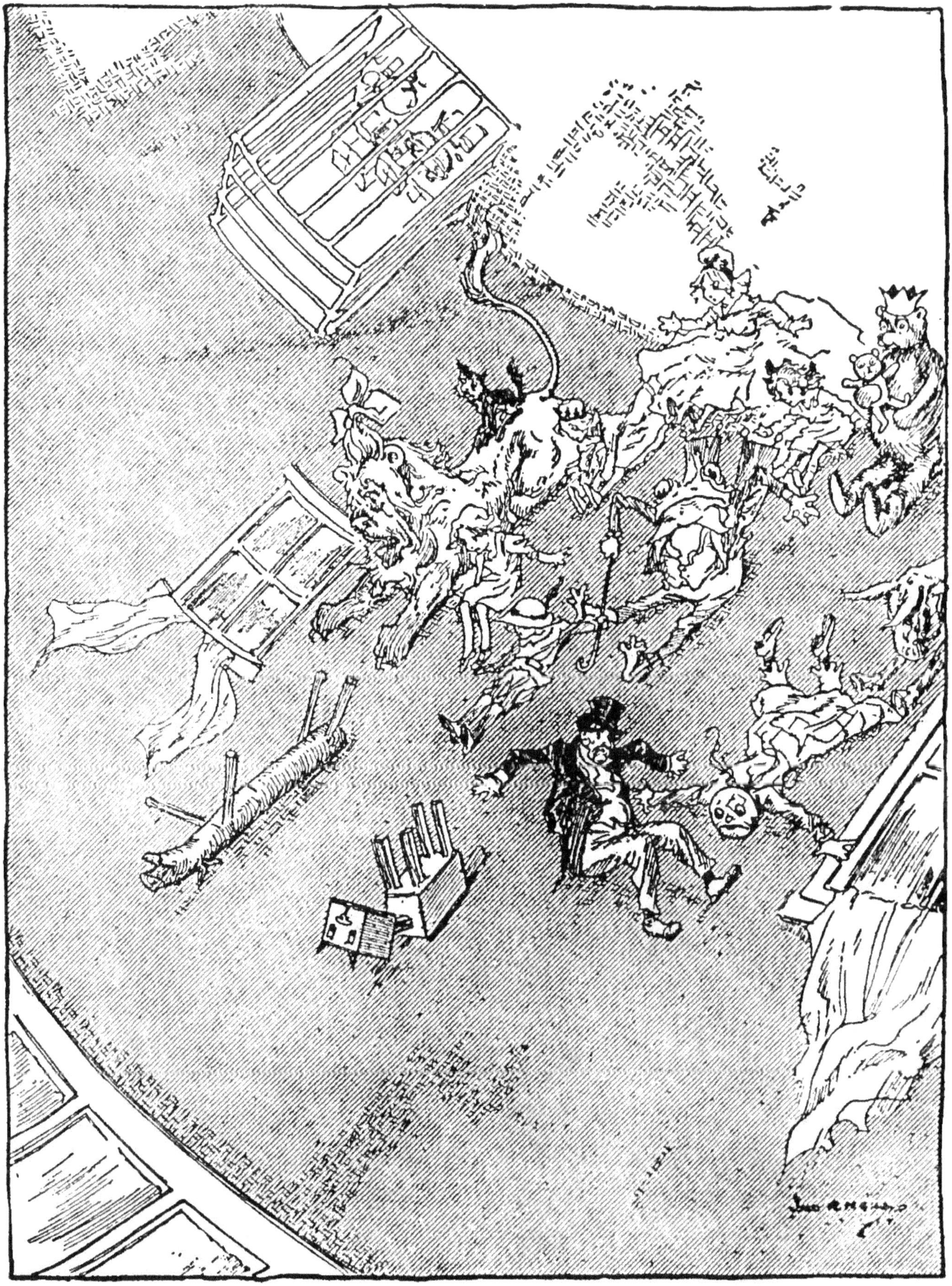

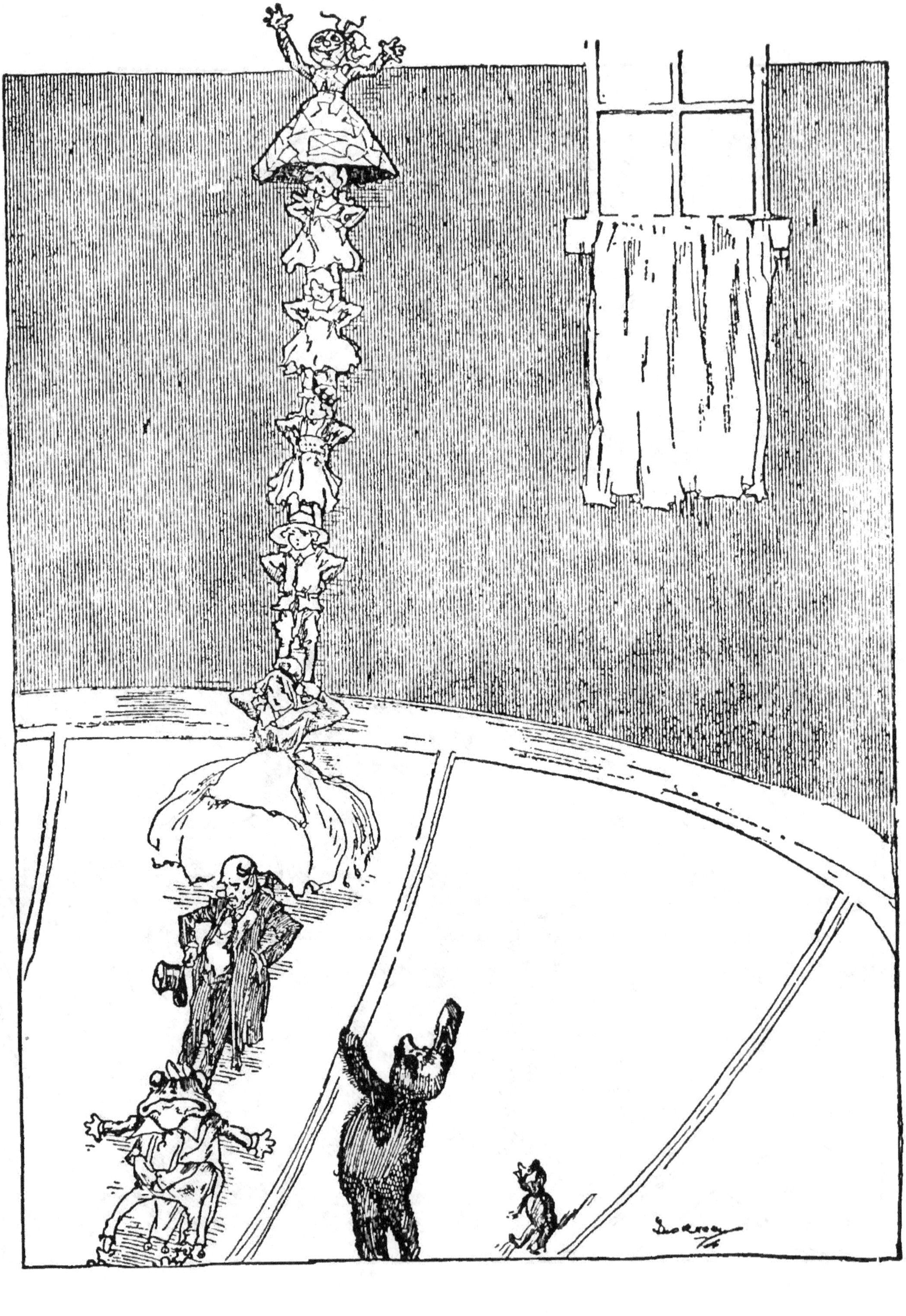

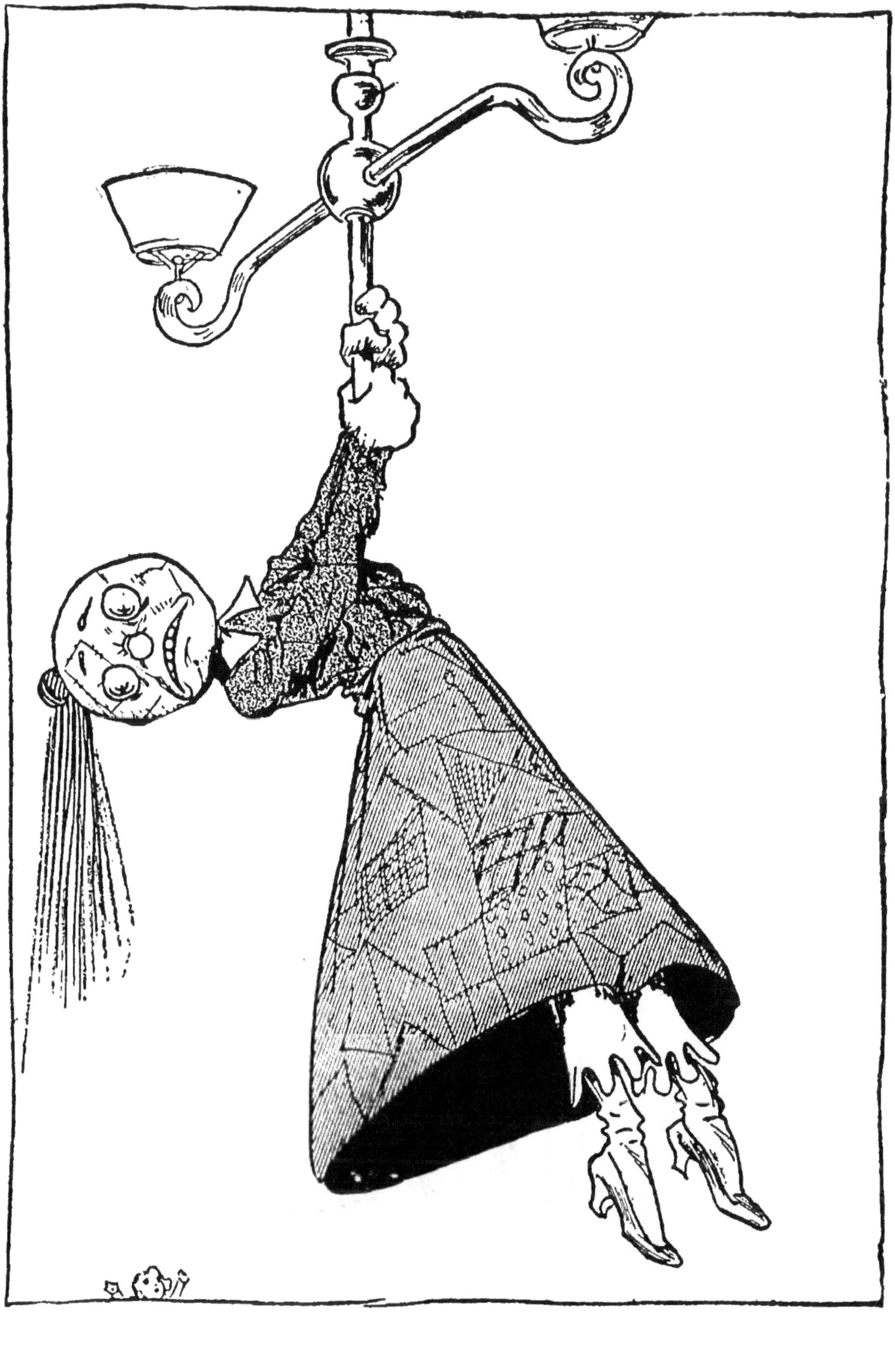

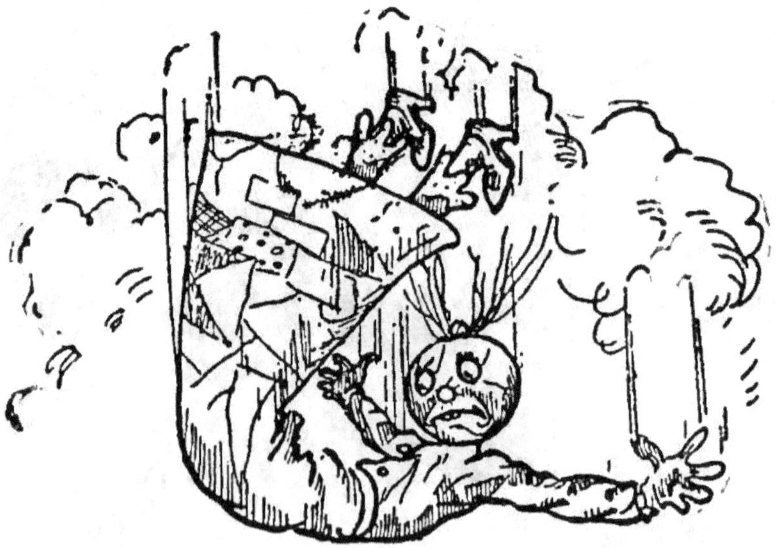

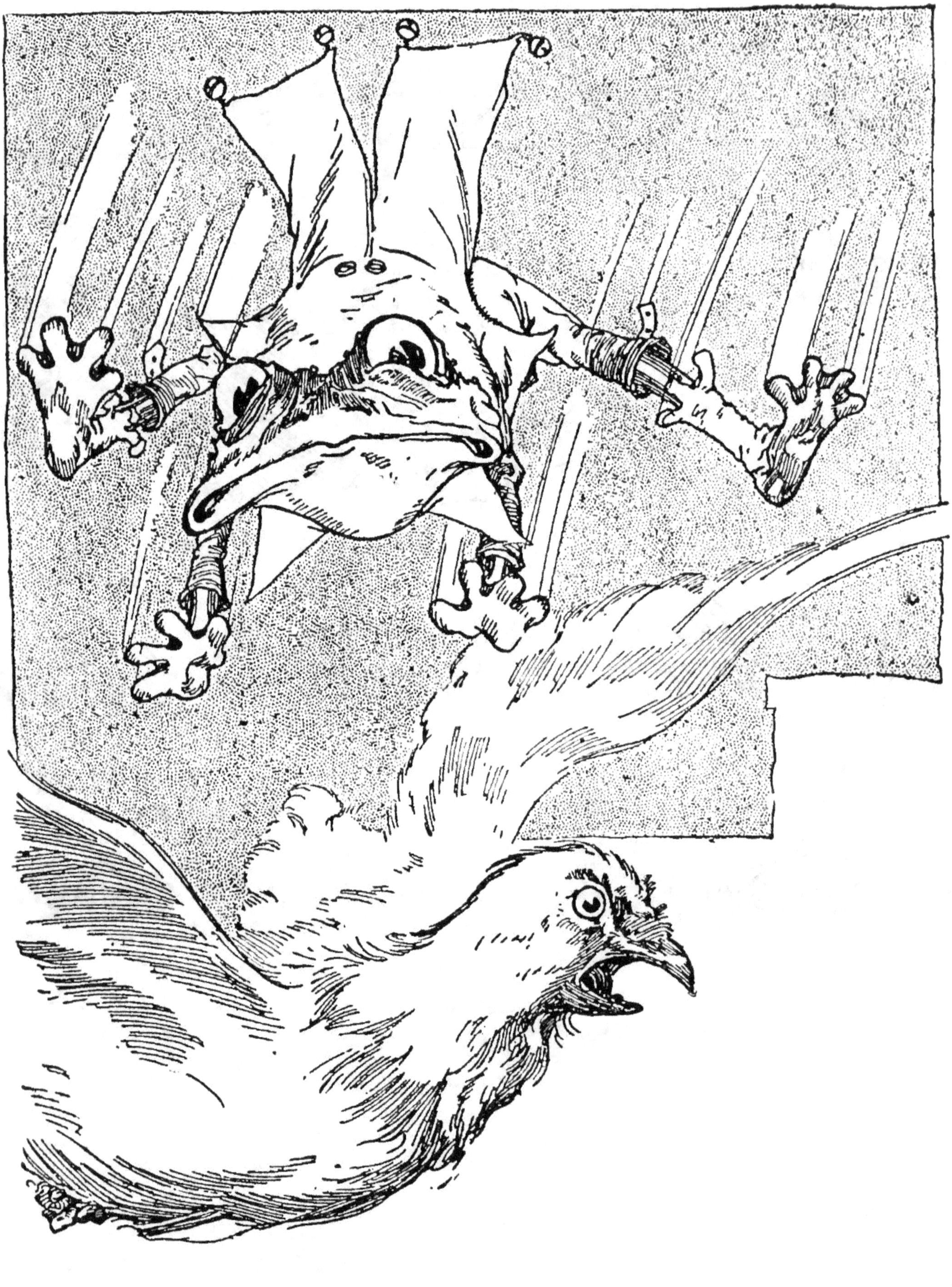

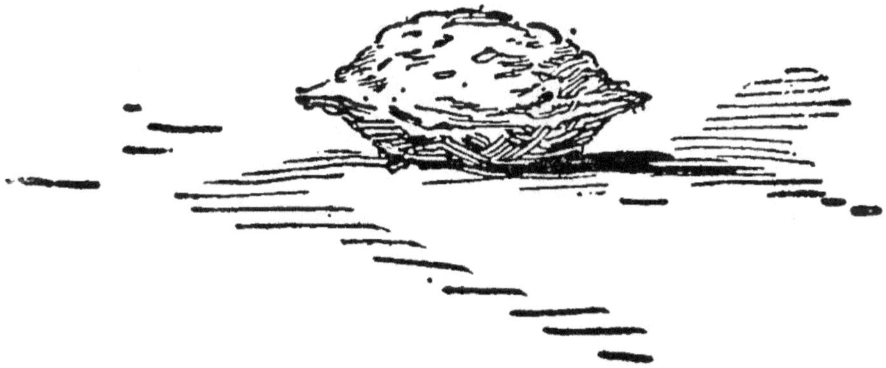

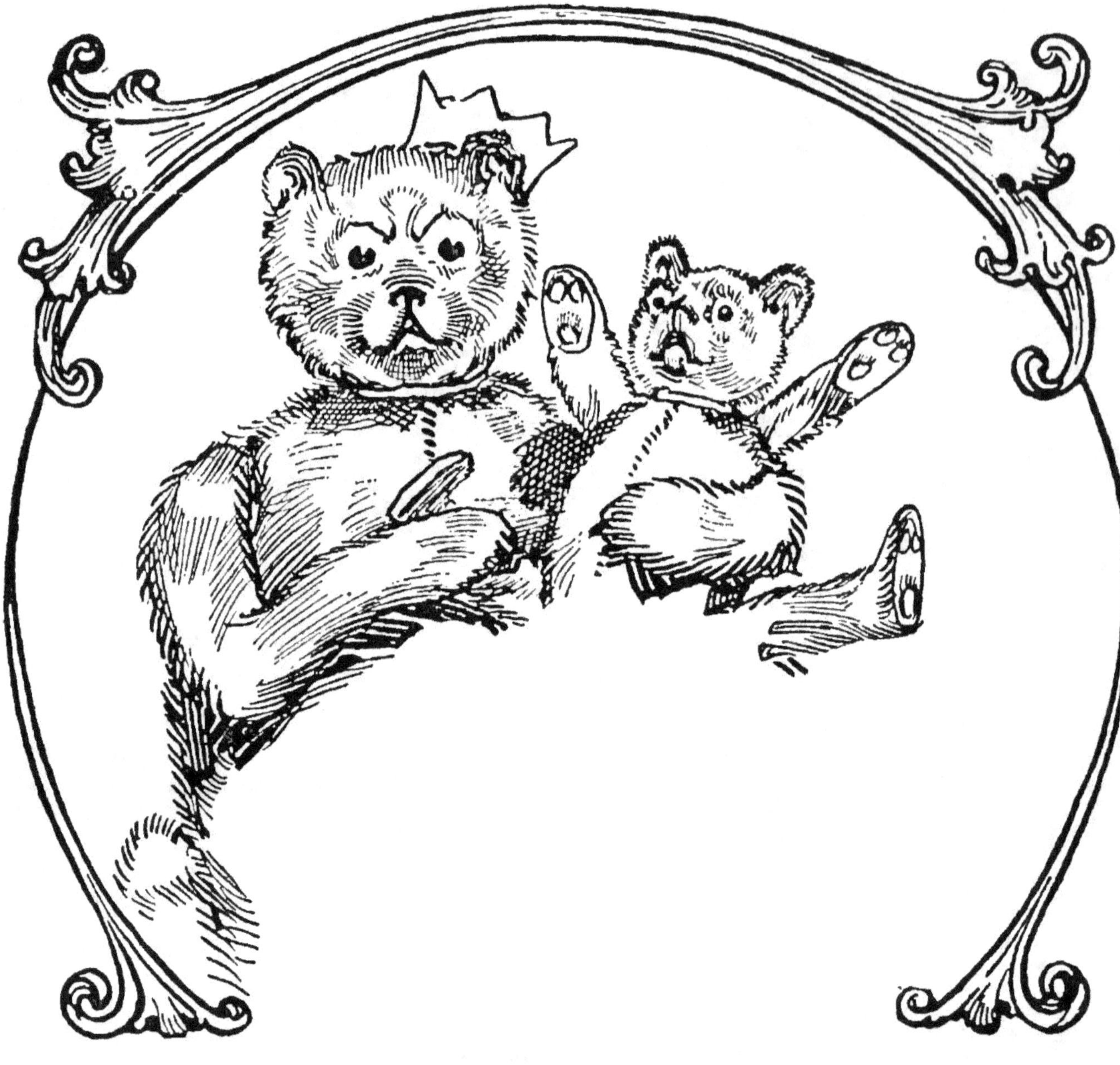

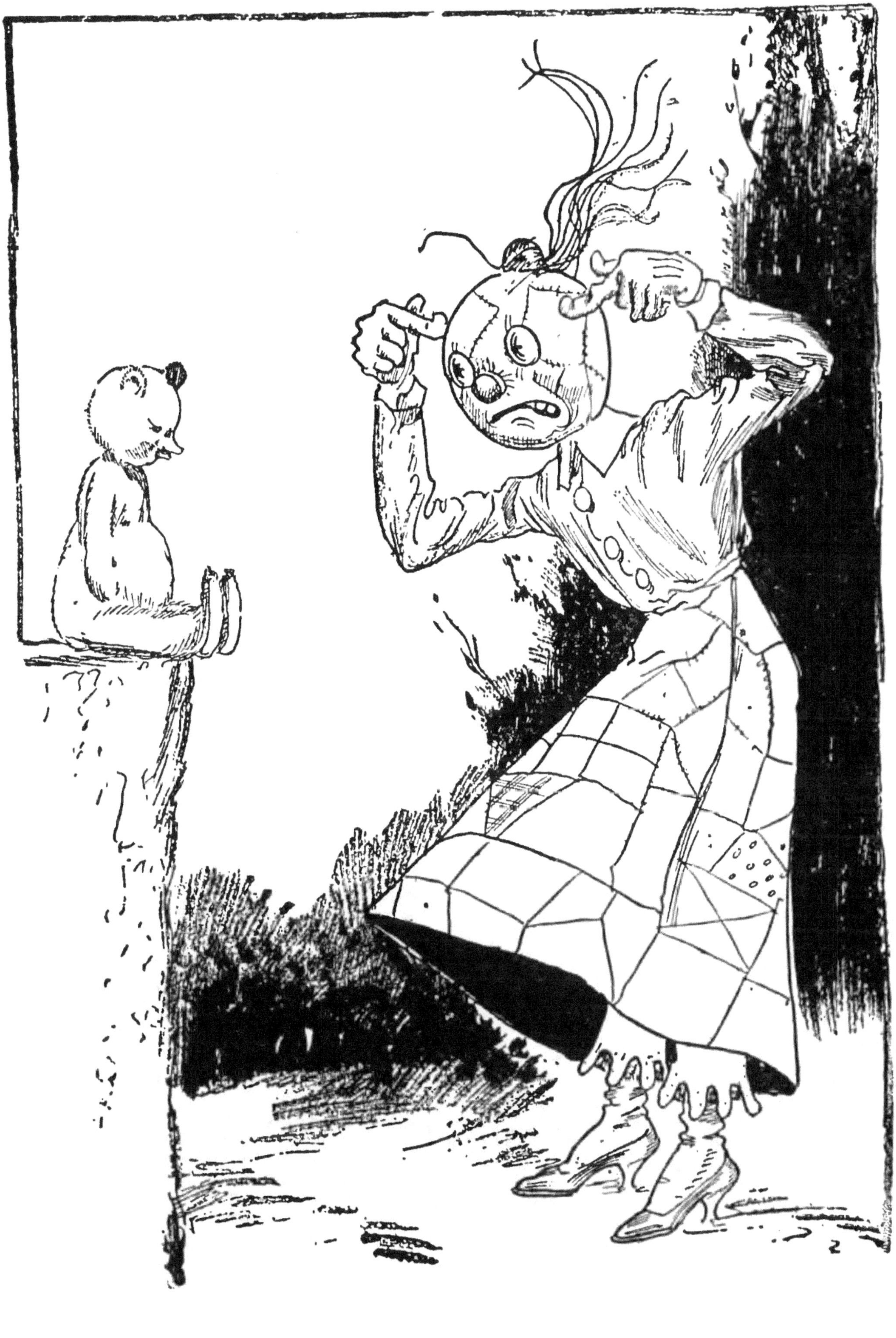

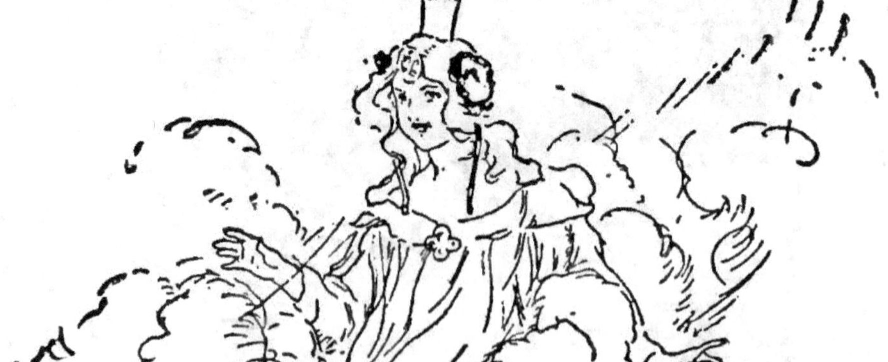

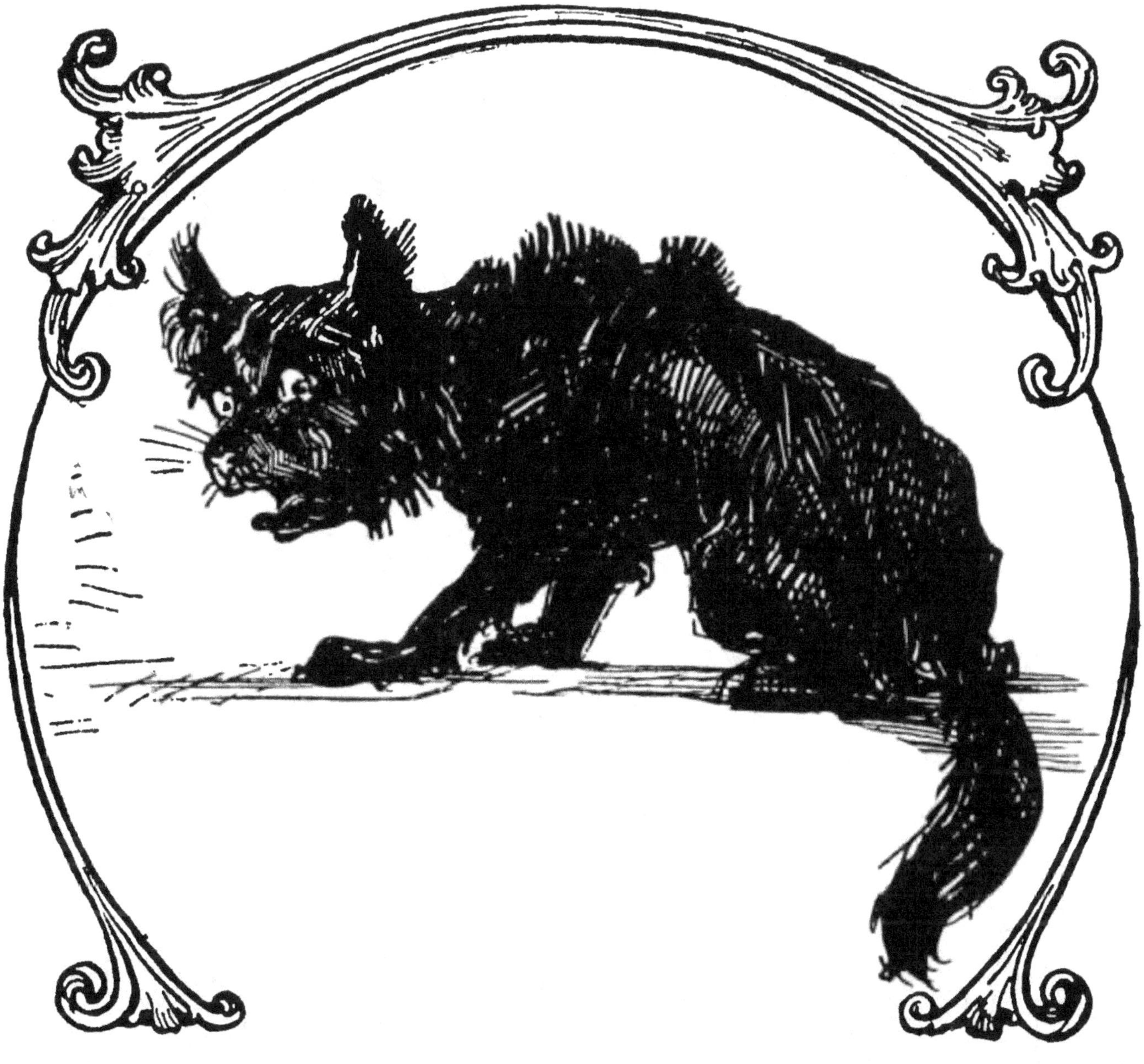

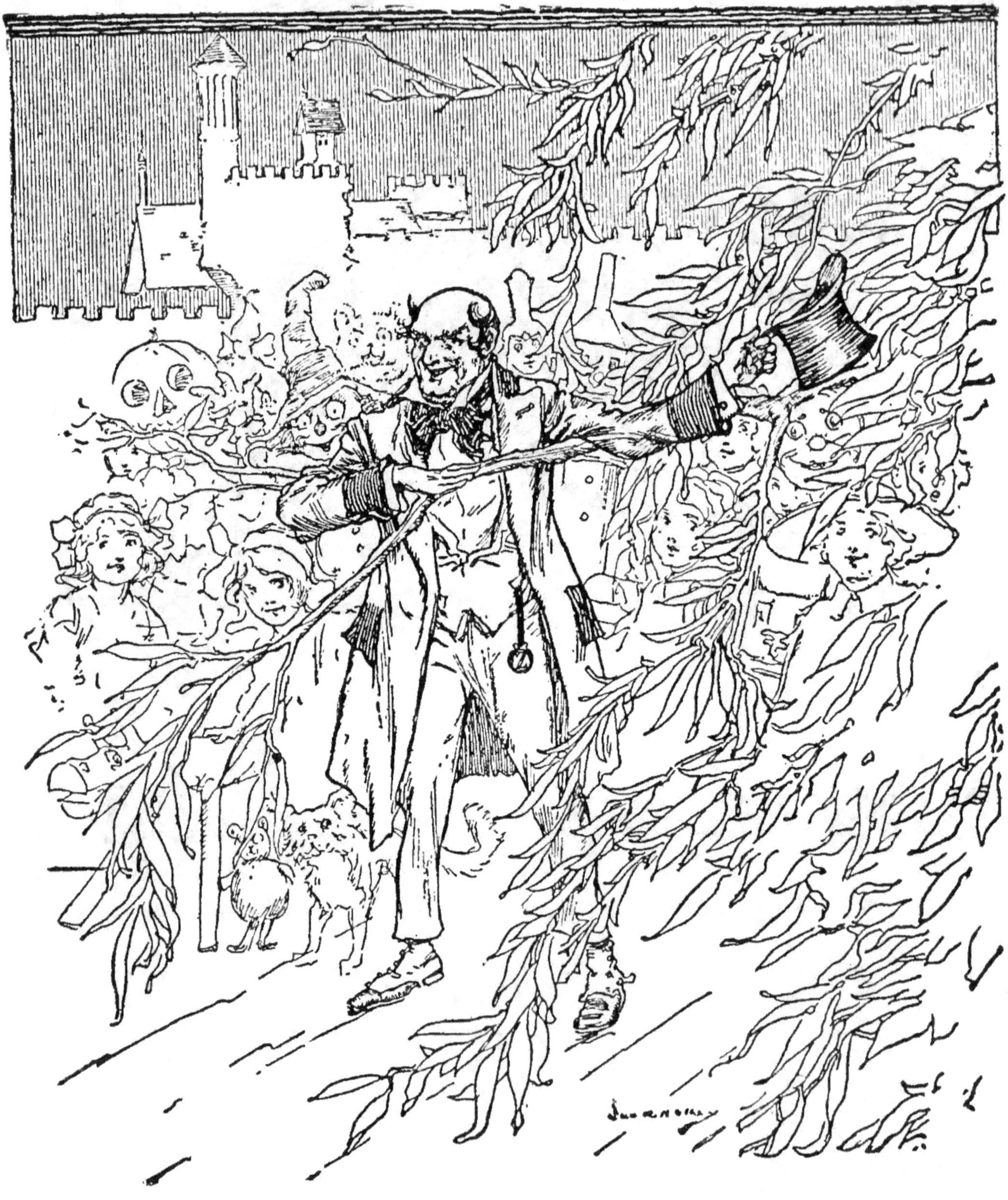

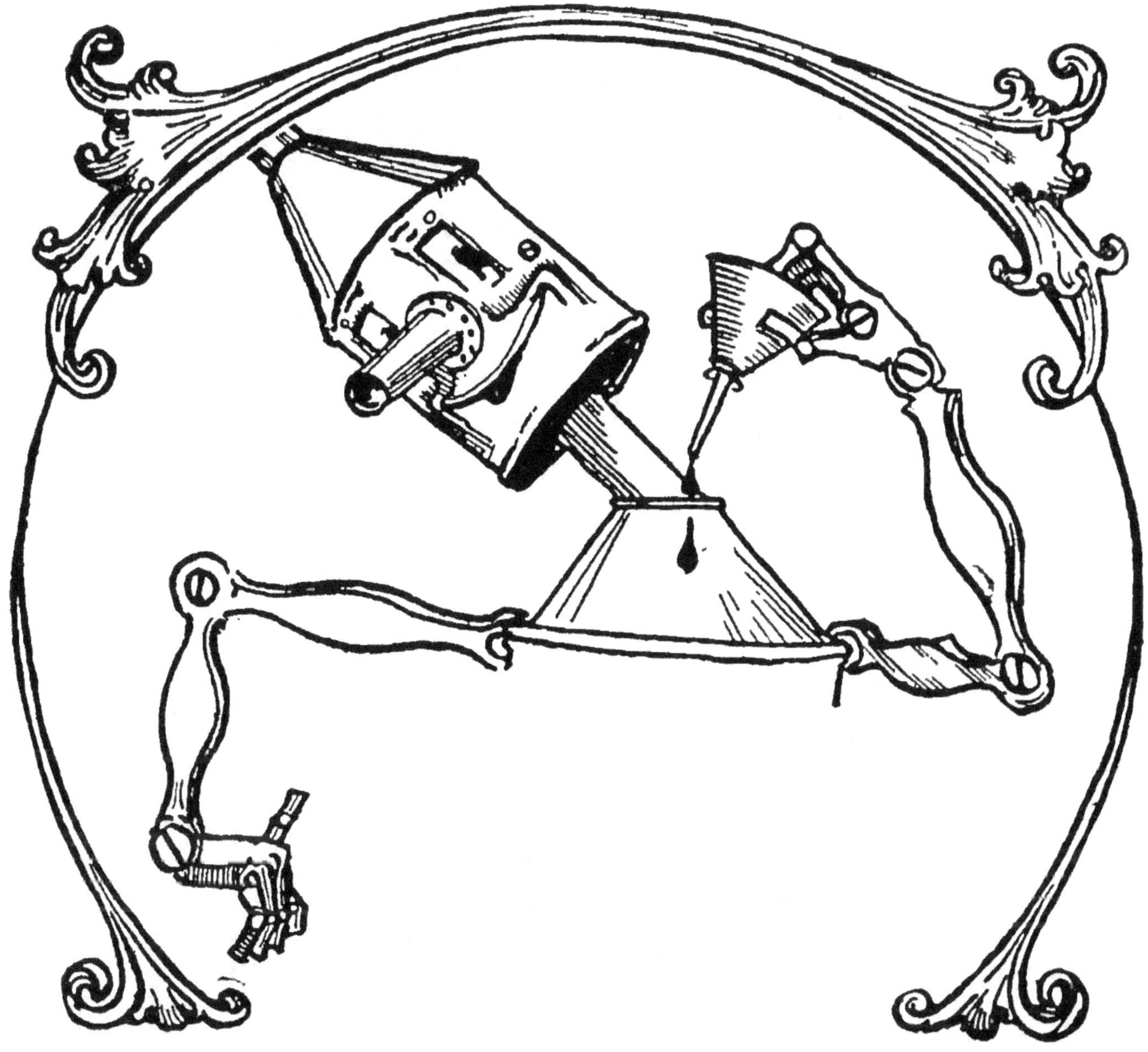

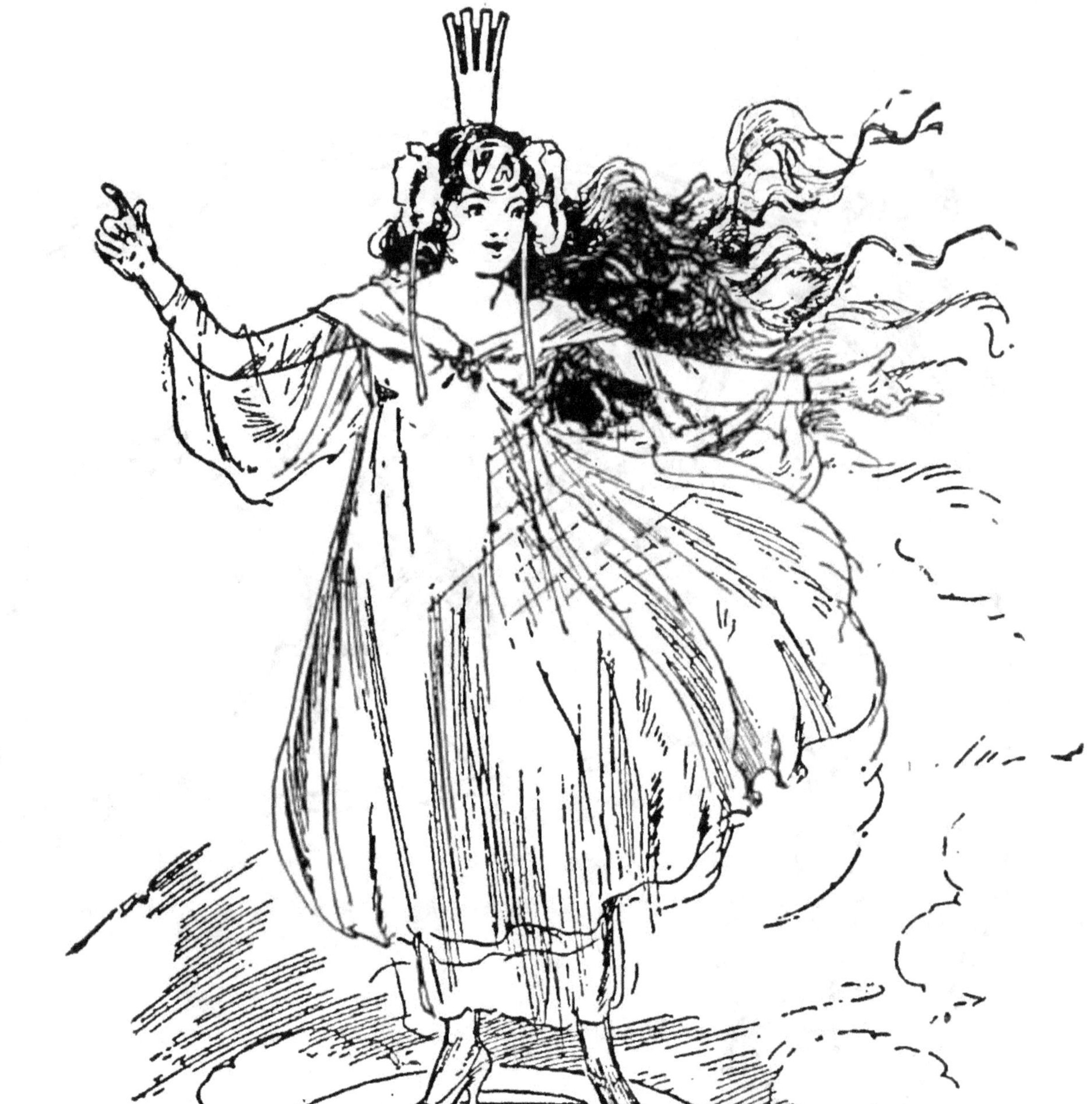

THE
END

www.ingramcontent.com/pod-product-compliance
Lightning Source LLC
Chambersburg PA
CBHW081118180526
45170CB00008B/2908